THE CRITICAL ROLE ... SUPREME C...

In this revealing ... scholar illumina... Court and explodes the ... ...tment of Justices. Among these ill-founded notions is "the myth of the surprised President," which holds that Justices often turn away from the policies of those who appointed them. Quite the contrary, says Tribe; Presidents usually get exactly what they want from the persons they choose. Nor does "the myth of the spineless Senate" survive scrutiny. History demonstrates that in fact the Senate has not acted as a mere rubber stamp for the President; it has rejected almost one out of every five nominees to the Court. As the author states, "Picking judges is too important a task to be left to any President."

GOD SAVE THIS
HONORABLE COURT

"A valuable book."—*ABA Journal*
"Succinct and authoritative."—*Publishers Weekly*
"Timely and effective . . . a valuable offering."
—*Kirkus Reviews*

LAURENCE H. TRIBE has taught at Harvard Law School since the age of twenty-seven, and holds Harvard's only chair in Constitutional Law. *Time* magazine named him one of the country's ten best law professors. The *National Law Journal* called him one of America's hundred most powerful lawyers in public or private life. His treatise *American Constitutional Law* received the Coif Award in 1980 for the most outstanding legal writing in the nation, and is widely said to be the leading modern work on the subject. Author of twelve other books and over ninety articles, and a frequent expert witness before Congress, Tribe also has won many important Supreme Court victories.

GOD
SAVE THIS
HONORABLE
COURT

_How the Choice of
Supreme Court Justices
Shapes Our History_

LAURENCE H. TRIBE

A MENTOR BOOK

NEW AMERICAN LIBRARY

NEW YORK AND SCARBOROUGH, ONTARIO

Published by arrangement with Random House, Inc.

Library of Congress Catalog Card Number: 86-61327

First Mentor Printing, October, 1986

1   2   3   4   5   6   7   8   9

PRINTED IN THE UNITED STATES OF AMERICA

Preface

The subject of this book—how the choice of Supreme Court Justices invisibly shapes our lives, and how that process of choosing Justices has both shaped and been shaped by America's past—is of enduring significance. Indeed, the untold story of how the selection of our Justice has helped chart the course of American history is both fascinating in its own right and vital for a self-governing people to understand. But the telling of that tale seemed to me especially timely in 1984, not only because of the fateful prophecies so long associated with the book named after that year but also because the presidential election posed so sharply the problem to which this book is addressed.

The choice that the American electorate made so resoundingly on November 6, 1984, reflected many of the public's concerns: among them, the personalities of the candidates, the budget deficit, the economy, the degree to which government should actively redistribute wealth, and how much of our resources we should spend on the military. But it is unlikely that the election reflected, in any decisive way, the considered views of more than a handful of the American people about the sorts of Justices they would want a reelected President Regan or a newly elected President Mondale to nominate. Walter Mondale's efforts to make such nominations a voting issue in a campaign dominated by talk of bombs and budgets may have affected a few voters, but hardly enough to matter one way or another. Yet, as I thought about how much more might in fact be at stake in such nominations than in nearly *anything* else that might be done—or undone—by the President who took the fiftieth oath of office on January 20, 1985, I became convinced that a book like this one was long overdue. Few political histories of Supreme Court appointments and their impact have been written, and those that exist are not the work of anyone steeped in constitutional law either as a scholar of the subject or as an advocate before the Court. The need I saw was for a book that lawyers and non-lawyers alike could readily follow, but one informed by the perceptions that only a thorough familiarity with the law could provide.

Having begun work on such a book long before, I was inspired to accelerate its completion not only by the impending election but also a public address delivered at the University of Minnesota by a sitting Justice, William H. Rehnquist, on October 19, 1984. In that speech made virtually on the eve of the presidential election, Justice Rehnquist reassured the nation that Presidents have enjoyed only "partial success" when seeking to "pack" the Supreme Court with nominees who would carry the President's perspective into the judicial branch, but added that he saw "no reason in the world why a President should not" *try*. I found myself in disagreement with the overall thrust of Justice Rehnquist's remarks, and sensed that those remarks could well serve, however unintentionally, to lower the public's guard, and lessen the Senate's vigilance, when the time came to review the next nomination, or indeed the next batch of nominations. I was further inspired by what seemed to me the quite naïve prescription offered by Judge Irving Kaufman, of the United States Court of Appeals for the Second Circuit, who urged, in a December 1984 *New York Times Magazine* article entitled "Keeping Politics Out of the Court," that Presidents should resist the temptation to inject their ideology into the Supreme Court through their nominations. Disagreeing in part with Justice Rehnquist, Judge Kaufman took the view that Presidents can indeed mold the Court in their image with substantial success, but that public trust in an independent judi-

ciary is threatened unless Presidents by and large make
more neutral criteria of proven excellence the dominant
guide to their use of the nomination power.

To me, any such notion flew in the face of an unavoidable political reality: Presidents will not suddenly
sacrifice one of their major ways to make a lasting
impact. Equally troublesome, the notion that Justices
should be chosen on neutral criteria of quality depended
to an unhealthy degree on, and could only reinforce, an
illusion about how "neutral" a Justice, or those who
nominate and either confirm or reject him or her, can
be. I saw a need to debunk at least two myths at
once—the myth that no one need fear a President's
Court-packing because Presidents regularly guess wrong
about, and are surprised by, the views and votes of
their Supreme Court nominees; and the myth that it
would be possible and desirable to choose Justices solely
in terms of the intellectual acumen with which they can
"decode" the mysteries of the Constitution's language
and history, without reference to their own beliefs about
society. People need to understand, it seemed to me,
why those who interpret and enforce the Constitution
simply cannot avoid choosing among competing social
and political visions, and why it is that those choices
will reflect *our* values—the diverse values of all those
who might read this book—only if we peer closely
enough, and probe deeply enough, into the outlooks of
those whom our Presidents name to sit on the Supreme
Court.

As this preface may already have made plain, much of
what this book contains represents the culmination of
more years of research and of reflection about the Supreme Court and its role than I care to confess. Thus I
cannot hope to trace here all the roots of the ideas that
appear in these chapters—or to allocate credit or blame
among the many who share indirect responsibility for the
thoughts I have expressed in all that follows. But I can
thank my good friend Bob Shrum for suggesting in
1983, and for urging even more insistently last fall, that
my ideas on this subject be expressed *soon*, and in a
nontechnical form accessible to a wide readership. And

I can thank two other friends and associates for the extraordinary research assistance that completing this book so soon after the November 1984 election required— Brian Koukoutchos, who received his J.D. from Harvard Law School in 1983, and Ronald Klain, who will receive his Harvard Law School degree in 1987, but who has already displayed a legal and political acumen rare in a beginning law student. To Brian Koukoutchos in particular I must express a special debt of thanks for his tireless and insightful assistance in ably crosschecking, lucidly editing, and carefully organizing far more material than I could possibly have marshaled and polished on my own in the pressured schedule I set for myself. To Rob Cowley, my editor at Random House, and to Alan Dershowitz, the friend and colleague who put me in touch with Rob, I also express my deep gratitude. To my exceptional assistant Leslie Sterling and my excellent secretary Robin Mesch—who in their other lives are, respectively, a talented rock singer and an aspiring commodities trader—go special thanks for helping to ensure that this book will be readable by nonspecialists and for making this ambitious project a pleasure instead of a pain. And to my extraordinary wife, Carolyn, and my terrific children, Mark and Kerry, go the gratitude that all three of them so richly deserve—not only for enduring *me* throughout this hectic time, but also for providing sounding boards that did far more than permit me to bounce ideas back and forth, but often reshaped and refined those ideas in mid-flight. Because my children, and the generation they represent, have even more at stake in the choice of future Justices than my contemporaries and I do, it seems especially fitting that they should have shared in the predictable effort, and the perhaps less predictable fun, that finishing this book has represented.

—Laurence H. Tribe
Cambridge, Massachusetts
January 1985

Contents

Prologue

THE GREYING OF
THE COURT

The heavy curtains part and the robed figures emerge to take their seats. The Marshal calls out, in a ritual that dates to the Court's very first meeting in 1790, "Oyez, oyez, oyez! All persons having business before the honorable, the Supreme Court of the United States, are admonished to draw near and give attention, for the Court is now sitting. God save the United States and this Honorable Court!"

But on this occasion, as on dozens before it, there is a notable emptiness in the chamber. One of the great high-backed chairs remains unfilled, and for the ninety-third time in American history a Justice has left the Surpreme Court of the United States.

This scene is more likely today than at any other time in recent memory. As a result of good health and good fortune, today's Surpreme Court is the first ever to have a majority of members over age seventy-six. If none of the current Justices meets with ill fate or chooses to retire, on November 3, 1986—almost two years to the day after Ronald Reagan's reelection—these eight men and one woman will become the oldest Surpreme Court in our nation's history. On that date, with an average age of seventy-two, the Justices will pass the previous record holders, the Supreme Court of the mid-1930s which gave Franklin Delano Roosevelt so much trouble that they were dubbed "the nine old men." Before the next presidential election, five of the Justices will be eighty or older.

There is no reason to assume that these Justices will

not be with us into the 1990s. According to the actuarial data, the five oldest Justices still have an average life expectancy of seven years, which could put them on the Court well past the Constitution's bicentennial in 1987. And although the work is strenuous, history suggests that the Justices might better serve than retire: among the Justices who have retired from the Court after fifteen years of service, the average life expectancy after resignation is under four years. The work of the Court may prove more bracing than exhausting.

The Justices themselves have resisted any attempt to hasten their resignations and are reluctant to acknowledge that their ages make them any less qualified to serve. In 1983 a lawyer arguing an immigration case before the Court was seeking relief for a doctor who wanted to become a naturalized citizen. When asked by Justice Harry Blackmun if his client was still practicing, the lawyer responded, "No, he's not. He's seventy-five years old." Justice Blackmun, a week away from his seventy-fifth birthday at the time, quipped, "That's young!" drawing smiles from fellow Justices Thurgood Marshall, William Brennan, Lewis Powell, and Chief Justice Warren Burger—themselves all older than Harry Blackmun. Later Justice Blackmun called himself "disgustingly healthy" for a man his age.

This is not the first group of Justices to believe that they are "only as old as they feel." Oliver Wendell Holmes, Jr., who served on the Court until past his ninetieth birthday, is reported to have admired a young woman passing his house and sighed, "Oh, to be eighty again!" Two of our most famous Chief Justices, John Marshall and Roger Taney, served to ages eighty and eighty-seven, respectively. Indeed, more than two-thirds of our Chief Justices have not retired until reaching their midseventies. Other distinguished Justices—Louis Brandeis, Hugo Black, and Felix Frankfurter, to name just three—served to their eightieth year or beyond.

Nonetheless, the "Greying of the Court" is of importance for at least three reasons.

First, it should call to our attention the enormous and lasting impact that these nine Justices, the six

Presidents who nominated them, and the seven Senates that confirmed them have had on our Constitution and our lives. The power of those nine jurists to make and shape constitutional choices about our government, our laws, and our future has been dramatic. Long after Richard Nixon's 1968 campaign pledge of "law and order" has become a distant memory, the four Justices he nominated to the Supreme Court remain on the bench, deciding "law and order" issues such as the power of police to stop and search cars or the future of the death penalty, as well as such unrelated issues as the home use of videotape machines and the legal rights of unmarried couples who live together. So, too, when only a handful of members remain from the Senate that rejected Nixon's nomination of G. Harrold Carswell to the Court, the nation still experiences the freedom of choice on abortion first articulated by the Justice who was chosen in Carswell's place: Harry Blackmun. The greying of the Court—the constancy of seven of its members who predate such historical divides as Watergate or the fall of Saigon—tends to obscure the tangible results that change on the Court can have on our society. The prospect, and the peril, of constitutional choice through the choice of Justices is discussed in detail in this book.

Second, the greying of the Court nurtures several myths about the way in which the institution has developed historically and the way it operates. The Court's current age and stability over time obscure the fact that Justices (and Supreme Courts) are chosen; they do not, like Minerva, spring forth full grown and wise from our forefather's foreheads. Justices are in fact chosen by the President and the Senate together—no President can appoint anyone to the Court without first obtaining the "advice and consent" of the Senate. Yet there has arisen a myth of the spineless Senate, which says that Senates always rubberstamp nominations and Presidents always get their way.

Finally, the Court's constancy over time may lead some to believe that the Court is somehow bigger than its members, and beyond being reshaped by them. This is the myth of the surprised President, which holds that no matter how much care Chief Executives devote to selecting their judicial nominees, they are incapable of "packing" the Court with Justices who will think and vote the way the White House wants. Justice Rehnquist, in a speech delivered at the University of Minnesota just before the November 1984 election, revealed the power this myth has to distort our vision. Justices, he declared, "invariably come 'one at a time,' and each new appointee goes alone to take his place with eight colleagues who are already there." The Court, impervious to changes in its memberships, absorbs all newcomers who must join the institution alone, "no cohorts with him."

The problem with this image is that it is so often inaccurate. Almost two-thirds of all the Court's members have taken seats within one year of another new Justice, creating an entering class of sorts. Since contemporaneous nominations tend to be made by the same President (and often one different from the one who made the previous choices), this "cohort" effect may be accentuated. Several times three or more Justices have joined the Court within one year. And, on six occasions, two new Justices have been named by the President or confirmed by the Senate on the same day. In fact, Justice Rehnquist himself was nominated to the Court on the same day as Judge Lewis Powell, with the two approved by the Senate only four days apart.

Today's greyed Court should not deflect our attention from the fact that enormous changes can occur there, changes that can produce major differences in constitutional outcomes. For example, 1922 nominees George Sutherland and Pierce Butler—named to the Court only eighty days apart—were the backbone of the anti—New Deal Court of the 1930's.

The donning of judicial robes and the taking of the appointed seat are not the powerful solvents of intellectual bias that some would have us believe. The ties that bind Justices to their previous experience and attitudes are not so easily dissolved. Presidents can and do change the Court's direction by changing its membership.

That power is of great significance to each and every one of us, for the most basic ingredients of our day-to-day lives are sifted and measured out by the Surpreme Court. When parents send their children to parochial schools, when men and women buy contraceptives, when workers organize a union, when friends share their intimate secrets in a telephone conversation without fear that others are listening, they enjoy rights and opportunities that would not exist if the Surpreme Court had not secured them for us.

Since fundamental choices about what sort of society we wish to become turned on *who* sits on the Court, the aging of the Justices signals a potential constitutional revolution in the making. Not since F.D.R. appointed seven Justices in four years has the nation faced the prospect of so drastic a change as it does today in the arbiter of our Constitution. Almost inevitably a bench filled with older Justices leads to a spate of appointments that can radically reshape the Court. The first "old Court" in our nation's history, the Surpreme Court of 1828 with an average age of sixty-three, was rocked by six nominations by President Andrew Jackson over the course of his two terms. Similarly, when the Court's average age neared sixty-nine in the spring of 1861, a major change awaited. Within the three-year period that followed, Abraham Lincoln named five Justices of his choosing. But the oldest Court prior to the one Roosevelt faced was the 1909 Court, which President William Howard Taft encountered. In just one term, Taft filled six vacancies—still the record for one term of a President.

A grey Supreme Court is a Surpreme Court ripe for this type of drastic overhaul. Choices will be made that are not reversible until another historic opportunity presents itself. Since the average tenure of a Supreme Court Justice is about fifteen years, any selections made today—or at any point in the next four to eight years—will shape that institution into the twenty-first century. A greyed Surpreme Court is thus a sort of Halley's Comet in our constitutional universe: a rare apparition arriving only once in each lifetime, burning intensely in our legal firmament for a brief period before returning to the deep space of constitutional history.

The relative tranquillity of only two Surpreme Court appointments in the past decade and a half—those of Justices John Paul Stevens and Sandra Day O'Connor—has turned our attention away from the important constitutional choices that must be made when filling positions on the nation's highest court. Not since 1826, when six of the Court's seven Justices had served together for fifteen years, has the Supreme Court's membership been so stable for so long. But today's grey Court means that this lull is only the calm before the constitutional storm that surely lies ahead. The appointment process has proceeded at a relaxed pace over the past quarter centry as the Court has grown older, producing only about half as many new Justices as were added to the Court in the first quarter of this century. Sometime in this decade we will be tossed into the turbulent process that has gripped this nation in the past. This book is about that process—its possibility and its promise, its pitfalls and its potential for shaping the course of law and politics in our republic.

Chapter One

HOW THE SUPREME COURT AFFECTS OUR LIVES

Those who are chosen to sit on the Supreme Court of the United States do more than fix its course as an institution: they exert a powerful, if often unseen and rarely understood, impact on nearly every aspect of our lives. The final words of the traditional proclamation with which the Marshal of the Supreme Court opens each session are "God save *the United States* and this Honorable Court." Just what *is* the connection between Court and country? Although it is the only one of our three branches of government that provides a written statement of its reasons every time it makes a decision, the Supreme Court remains something of a mystery. Yet there is a clear and fundamental link between the United States of America and its Supreme Court—between the best-known and most powerful judicial body in the world and the lives of the two hundred million citizens whom the Court's Marshal invites "to draw near and give their attention."

The Supreme Court has not always been considered an especially significant national institution. In its early years the Court did not have the stature of its sister branches, the Congress and the Presidency, and to be appointed a Justice, while certainly an honor of some degree, was not sufficiently prestigious to entice many of the nation's leading figures. The Court did not have its own building until this century—it used to meet in a dank crypt beneath the old Senate chamber, described by the *New York Tribune* in March of 1859 as a "potato hole of a place . . . a queer room of small dimensions

1

and shaped overhead like a quarter section of a pumpkin shell." In the Court's early terms it was not unusual for several Justices to miss arguments and conferences because they felt that they had better things to do. When the seminal case of *Marbury v. Madison* was argued in 1803, only three of the Court's six Justices bothered to attend.

With such a beginning, it is not hard to understand how the Supreme Court came to be known as "the least dangerous branch" of our government. The Congress can reach out to make changes in our lives by taxing us and passing laws on almost any subject. The President is the single most powerful figure in the country—he commands the armed forces, directs national policy, and enforces the laws. The Supreme Court, by contrast, can only *react* to the controversies that are brought before it by litigants. If people or prosecutors choose not to take a matter to court and appeal it all the way to the top, the Justices of the highest court in the land are powerless even to *say*, let alone *do*, anything about it. Therein lies the key to what Alexander Hamilton called "the natural feebleness of the judiciary." It is tempting to conclude that this low-profile institution is not all that important, and that it doesn't really matter *who* sits on the Court. Yet nothing could be further from the truth.

In the two centuries that have passed since the Supreme Court's first Marshal said his first "Oyez," the Court's importance has grown by a slow but steady accretion, until today there is hardly an aspect of American life that has not been touched by the hands of our highest tribunal. A President resigns, a gargantuan corporation disintegrates, a frightened but hopeful child marches to school with her military escort past a hostile crowd, all because nine black-robed figures in Washington have gleaned new wisdom from an old and hallowed document. The sweep of the Supreme Court's influence is so vast that it cannot be grasped by the eye. A comprehensive tour of that immense landscape is not possible here; but a brief sampling of its rich and varied terrain can convey a sense of the Court's pervasive influence.

A GOVERNMENT OF LAWS

When the Framers of our Constitution traveled to Philadelphia in 1787 to form a new government, they carried with them two insights of fundamental importance. The first, born of the colonial experience and the recent war for independence, was that the concentration of all government power in the same hands was the very definition of tyranny. The second, gained during the brief life of the regime established by the Articles of Confederation, was that a weak central government was inadequate to the task of ruling a vast and varied nation of thirteen states jealous of their prerogatives.

The method the Framers chose to resolve this dilemma was the distribution of power into three more or less distinct branches—legislative, executive, and judicial. The common denominator of the three was and is the law; in simple but still informative terms, the first writes the laws, the second enforces them, and the third resolves disputes under them. The *people* of the nation remain the sovereign, and all the coercive power they have delegated to the government may be exercised only pursuant to the law. Thus, in accord with Article VI of the Constitution, every legislator "and all executive and judicial officers" in American government, from a traffic court judge to the Chief Justice of the United States, from the lowliest ensign to the Commander in Chief, swears not an oath to obey any monarch but an oath to "support this Constitution." The highest loyalty is owed not to any person, no matter how exalted, but to an *idea* made into *law*. As Chief Justice John Marshall declared in *Marbury v. Madison,* ours is "a government of laws, and not of men." In that same case, he underscored the pivotal role of the judiciary in such a regime: "It is emphatically the province and duty of the judicial department to say what the law is."

In a nation that has come to be the greatest law factory the world has ever known, the power to interpret the law is an awesome one. Even a hundred and fifty years ago the French political analyst Alexis de

Tocqueville observed that "scarcely any political question arises in the United States that is not resolved, sooner or later, into a judicial question." The natural result is that the Supreme Court is eventually caught up in most of the great controversies of any given age, a situation that prompted Justice Holmes's remark that the only peace ever found at the Supreme Court is the uneasy stillness one finds at the eye of a hurricane.

A dramatic example of how most political questions eventually present themselves for judicial resolution—and of the fact that no man is above the law—is *United States v. Nixon*. In the autumn of 1973 Watergate Special Prosecutor Archibald Cox served President Richard Nixon with a subpoena for certain tape recordings made in the Oval Office. When the district court and the court of appeals upheld that subpoena, Nixon fired Cox and a number of other Justice Department officials, but eventually turned over the requested tapes to the district judge for inspection in the privacy of the court's chambers. The following spring, the new Special Prosecutor, Leon Jaworski, subpoenaed more tapes in connection with his prosecution of Nixon's former Attorney General, John Mitchell, and former White House aides John Ehrlichman and H. R. Haldeman. President Nixon flatly denied the subpoena and the Special Prosecutor took the matter on an expedited appeal to the Supreme Court, which ruled unanimously in the Special Prosecutor's favor. The eight sitting Justices—including three Nixon appointees—rejected the President's assertion of an absolute "executive privilege" to withhold presidential documents, and declared that a President, too, must obey a judicially enforced subpoena because no one, not even the nation's Chief Executive, is above the law. Richard Nixon turned over the tapes—which contained the "smoking gun" evidence necessary to impeach him—and promptly resigned the office of President.

President Nixon was not the first occupant of the Oval Office who was forced to comply with a judicial order. In 1807 Chief Justice John Marshall, in his capacity as Circuit Justice for Virginia, convened a grand jury in Richmond to investigate accusations of treason made against former Vice President Aaron Burr by President Thomas Jefferson. The ever-colorful Burr, who had alienated Jefferson by almost gaining the Presidency for himself by a constitutional quirk when he was Jefferson's running mate in 1800, requested that a subpoena be issued to the President of the United States. Burr demanded that Jefferson appear before the grand jury and bring with him certain government correspondence and military orders. President Jefferson announced that he would turn over only what he wanted to, and nothing more. Chief Justice Marshall—who happened to be the President's cousin and longtime family rival—declared that since Jefferson was not an anointed king, he had to comply with the law just like any other man. An enraged Jefferson eventually produced the requested documents and the grand jury indicted Burr for treason. The fact that the jury acquitted Burr of the President's dubious charges is less important than the fact that the President of the United States was forced to comply with a judicial order just like any other citizen.

Chief Justice Marshall angered more than one President with his firm assertions of the Supreme Court's constitutional prerogatives. President Andrew Jackson is reputed to have reacted to a Supreme Court opinion with which he violently disagreed—but which did not purport to give orders to the Chief Executive—by saying, "John Marshall has made his decision; now let him enforce it." Whether Jackson actually said that or not, he plainly thought he could get away with repudiating the Court's authority. But the Supreme Court's authority is not so easily defied today. During the Korean War, President Truman ordered a federal takeover of the nation's steel mills for the stated purpose of preventing anticipated labor strikes against that strategic industry from disrupting the war effort. The Court invalidated the President's order on the ground that only the Congress has the power to seize property in the public interest, and in the Court's opinion Congress had not authorized the president's act. With the stroke of a pen the Supreme Court brought to heel the Commander in Chief, who did not even pause before acceding to the Court's judgment.

The Supreme Court's role in preserving our government of laws is played out not only on the grand stage of national affairs, but in more modest and mundane theaters as well. Edward Lawson, a San Diego business consultant who dressed eccentrically and wore his long hair in Caribbean "dreadlocks," was in the habit of going for long walks at all times of the day. He strolled only for his pleasure, and usually carried no identification with him. This practice ran afoul of the local police, who repeatedly arrested and jailed Lawson on the basis of a California law that permitted them to arrest anyone who failed to account for his activity and produce credible identification when stopped by an officer. On one occasion, Lawson was dragged out of a restaurant by police who claimed to be looking for a one-legged white man; Lawson has two legs and is black. In *Kolender v. Lawson*, the Supreme Court struck down the California law in 1983 because it vested virtually complete discretion in the hands of the police to determine what constituted "credible identification." A nation that prizes its liberties, the Court ruled, cannot tolerate such a delegation of unbridled power.

THE LIBERTIES OF US ALL

Edward Lawson's case is but one recent example of the ways in which even the Supreme Court's less dramatic decisions shape the fundamental liberties that we often take for granted. Other illustrations surround us. News commentators talk of how the Supreme Court broadened the power of public school officials to preserve order and safety when it gave a green light in 1985 to teachers and principals to search our children's lockers and lunch bags upon mere "reasonable" hunches that something may be amiss. Yet little or nothing was said about how the Supreme Court, in that same case, emphatically and unanimously rejected the claim by school officials that, being stand-ins for us as parents, they should be entirely freed of the Constitution's ban on "unreasonable searches and seizures." Without a Supreme Court able and willing to say no to such extravagant claims by Big Brother, our lives would be changed beyond recognition. But like the goldfish that does not know that it is wet, we go about our daily lives unaware of the pervasive influence that the Supreme Court's decisions have on all of us.

The Court's influence is profound because of its central role in delivering on the Constitution's promises. The authors of our Constitution undertook to secure conditions favorable to the pursuit of happiness. As Justice Louis Brandeis pointed out in 1928, when he dissented from the Court's opinion upholding wiretapping in *Olmstead v. United States*, the Framers "knew that only a part of the pain, pleasure and satisfaction of life are to be found in material things. They sought to protect Americans in their beliefs, their thoughts, their emotions and their sensations. They conferred, as against the government, the right to be let alone—the most comprehensive of rights and the right most valued by civilized men." The Fourth Amendment, for example, protects the "right of the People to be secure in their persons, houses, papers and effects against unreasonable searches and seizures." The Supreme Court first held over seventy years ago that this means evidence seized in an illegal search cannot be used against the person whose Fourth Amendment rights were violated; admitting such evidence at trial would put a judicial stamp of approval on official lawlessness. As Sophocles said, nobody has a more sacred obligation to obey the law than those who make and enforce it.

This so-called exclusionary rule has often been criticized for valuing the rights of criminals above those of law-abiding citizens. But those who wrote the Constitution's limitations on how suspects may be pursued obviously knew that taking those limits seriously—that is, *obeying* them rather than flouting them—would necessarily prevent some guilty people from being apprehended and convicted. The exclusionary rule simply makes that result more dramatic and visible than might some other rules—rules that successfully prevent illegal searches from occurring in the first place. But whatever its price, the exclusionary rule plainly protects the liberties of *all* of us.

No case proves this better than *Mapp v. Ohio*, the first instance in which the Supreme Court, in 1961, applied the exclusionary rule to the states in addition to the federal government. Dollree Mapp was a middle-class homeowner who rented out the first floor of her house to help make a living for herself. One May afternoon in 1957, the police arrived at her door and demanded to be let in. They said they were looking for a man who was wanted for questioning about a bombing. Miss Mapp called her attorney and then asked to see the search warrant. When the officers replied that they did not have one, she forbade them to enter her home and sent them away. Three hours later the police, still without a warrant, broke down the door to Miss Mapp's house and charged upstairs to her apartment. When she demanded to see a search warrant, the police waved a worthless piece of paper at her. Dollree snatched the paper and stashed it in her turtleneck sweater. The three policemen tackled her, handcuffed her, and rummaged under her clothing to retrieve what they falsely claimed to be a warrant. The officers then proceeded to tear up the place looking for anything they could find. In Miss Mapp's bedroom, the police found some books and pictures they considered obscene. Dollree testified that she was merely storing the items and other personal articles for a former tenant who had moved without leaving a forwarding address. Despite that fact, and the illegal and outrageous nature of the police invasion of her home, Miss Mapp was sentenced to one to seven years in prison on an obscenity charge. She traveled to Washington, D.C., to hear her case argued before the Supreme Court while she was out on bail. The Court overturned her conviction and set her free.

Thus some fundamental rights that we take for granted exist only because the Supreme Court has said so. By the same token, some less visible government invasions of our privacy, to which many law-abiding people would strenuously object, have been endorsed by the Court. Although the Justices' reading of the Fourth Amendment's search warrant requirement protects us from midnight police raids on our homes, their reading does not prevent the police from examining all of our bank accounts and personal checks, or learning all of the phone numbers that we dial. The Supreme Court in the 1970s ruled that the government can make banks turn over all of the records of any depositor's financial transactions, and can obtain from the telephone company lists of all of the numbers any customer calls, without a search warrant and without any notice to the citizen whose trust has been betrayed. Although Supreme Court decisions thus leave us with no legally protected expectation of privacy in the checks processed by our banks, nor even in the digits we dial into the telephone company's computers, we do enjoy the Constitution's legal protection when we expect that the conversations we have on those phone calls will be private: the Supreme Court in 1967 expanded the privacy rights of us all by requiring the government to obtain a search warrant before tapping a telephone. Thus we are freer to call and converse without fear that someone is listening in on Big Brother's behalf, whether to gather personal secrets for extortion, to ferret out political dissent, or to detect ordinary wrongdoing.

If we choose to converse in the open, or even to mount a soapbox, a long line of Supreme Court decisions protects our right to criticize government policy and even to preach revolution—without risking a jail term, a fine, or any other penalty. In this same spirit the Court has held that a free government cannot silence even defamatory criticism by its citizens: such a government has nothing to fear from free and frank discussion. No "thought police" patrol the population looking for political heretics. Nor may the government dictate to us what is to be orthodox in matters of conscience and religious belief. The Court has ruled that the government may not compel schoolchildren to pray or to pledge allegiance to the flag, and may not structure such programs as public education and unemployment insurance in such a way that they even inadvertently impinge on a citizen's freedom to exercise his chosen religion. The Court has held, for instance, that unemployment compensation cannot be denied to a Jehovah's Witness because he was fired for refusing a transfer to a job building tank turrets; nor may Amish parents be compelled to send their children to school past the age of twelve.

Although they are less politically dramatic, our economic rights are also secure in significant part because of the Supreme Court's rulings. Margarita Fuentes bought household goods, as many of us must, on an installment plan. She had paid two-thirds of the amount due on her gas stove and stereo when a dispute arose over a service contract on the stove. The company that sold her the furnishings quickly sent a deputy sheriff and a truck to her home and carted the furnishings away, under a state law which allowed such repossession without requiring the creditor to show a judge or any other neutral official that the sales contract had been violated. Mrs. Fuentes would of course have a chance to prove at a subsequent trial that she had a right to stop payments, but in the meantime her stereo was gone and she had no way to cook her meals. So in 1972 the Supreme Court held in the case of *Fuentes v. Shevin* that a person's property rights may not be so cavalierly ignored—that the state must hold a preliminary hearing before allowing a creditor to repossess.

No one should assume that the Supreme Court need always strike down laws and executive actions in order to protect our liberties. On the contrary, sometimes the Court best guarantees our rights by deferring to, rather than overruling, the political branches. When the Supreme Court, from 1900 to 1937, struck down dozens of child labor laws, minimum wage laws, working condition regulations, and laws protecting workers' rights to organize unions, on the ground that such rules infringed on property rights and violated "liberty of contract," the only rights the Court really vindicated were the rights to be overworked, underpaid, or unemployed. The Court eventually reversed itself on these issues when it recognized that, in twentieth-century America, such laws are not intrusions upon human freedom in any meaningful sense, but are instead entirely reasonable and just ways of combating economic subjugation. In upholding a minimum wage law in the watershed case of *West Coast Hotel v. Parrish*, the Supreme Court concluded in 1937 that, in the light of "recent economic experience," such statutes were justified because they prevent "the exploitation of a class of workers in ways detrimental to their health and well being."

Naturally, in this imperfect world, the Supreme Court has not always guarded our liberties as jealously as it should. During the First World War and again in the McCarthy era, the Court often shrank from the affirmation of our rights to think and speak as we believe. And in the war hysteria following the bombing of Pearl Harbor, the Supreme Court in *Korematsu v. United States* upheld the imprisonment of thousands of Americans of Japanese ancestry who had committed no crime. In light of such lapses, some have argued that when it comes to protecting fundamental rights, the Supreme Court is essentially redundant: on most occasions the Congress and the President will adequately safeguard our rights, and in those difficult times when the political branches cannot be counted on, neither can the Court.

There is a sad kernel of truth in this argument, but the kernel is a small one. The argument's cynicism overlooks the fact that the moments when the political branches are perfectly in tune with the Bill of Rights, and the moments when even the judicial branch fails in its protective mission, add up to but a fraction of the republic's history. The vast bulk of the Court's work falls into the large grey area between these extremes, where there is no authoritarian Big Brother who threatens our freedom, but where the threat still comes from insensitive legislation, overreaching executive action, or the dogged pursuit of bureaucratic prerogatives. As Justice Brandeis reminded us long ago, "experience should teach us to be most on our guard to protect liberty when the government's purposes are beneficent. Men born to freedom are naturally alert to repel invasion of their liberty by evil-minded rulers. The greatest dangers to liberty lurk in insidious encroachment by men of zeal, well-meaning but without understanding." Nor can the national political branches be depended upon even in the best of times to stem encroachments on personal liberty occasionally committed by state and local, rather than federal, government. In such situations the federal judiciary is our best and often our only guardian.

PERSONAL CHOICES

Sometimes the decisions of the Supreme Court secure for us liberties so basic to our everyday lives that most people would be appalled to learn that the government officials we elect have ever tried to deny us those liberties. Mrs. Inez Moore lived in East Cleveland, Ohio, with her two grandsons, Dale and John. The boys were not brothers but cousins—John's mother had died before he was a year old and he was thereafter raised by his grandmother. In 1973 Mrs. Moore received a notice from the city that since John and Dale were cousins rather than brothers, her household did not meet the unusual and complicated definition of a "family" in the city's zoning ordinance. Because Mrs. Moore lived in a neighborhood that had been zoned for "single-family dwelling units," she was told by East Cleveland officials that her ten-year-old grandson John was an "illegal occupant" who must be removed. When Mrs. Moore refused to throw her grandson out of the only home he had ever known, the sixty-three-year-old woman was fined and sentenced to five days in jail.

The good news is that, in its 1977 decision of *Moore v. East Cleveland,* the Supreme Court overturned Mrs. Moore's conviction and ruled that although communities may enact ordinances to prevent overcrowding and reduce traffic congestion, the zoning power is not, in the words of Justice William Brennan, Jr., "a license to enact senseless and arbitrary restrictions which cut deeply into private areas of protected family life." The bad news is that only five Justices in all agreed with this sentiment while four members of the Court would have sent the grandmother to jail for the crime of providing a home for her motherless grandchild.

In addition to restricting efforts by the states to impose an orthodox model of the nuclear family, the Supreme Court has clamped down on laws that would dictate who shall form a family with whom. In the ironically named case of *Loving v. Virginia* in 1967, the Court struck down Virginia's miscegenation statute, declaring that government had no business telling black and white citizens that they may not marry one another.

Equal in importance to the freedom to choose a spouse is the freedom to decide whether one will have children. It is hard to imagine a decision more personal, more intimate, and more central to an individual's pursuit of happiness. Yet the elected governments of the states in which we live have often invaded this most private of realms. The strongest bulwark against such invasions is the Supreme Court, but it has not always been a staunch defender.

Tests for Intelligence Quotient, or I.Q., were taken very seriously in the early decades of this century, and they became an important tool for purging America of "mental defectives." Carrie Buck was a young woman with a child of allegedly feeble mind; both Carrie and her mother were also classified as mentally deficient on the basis of I.Q. tests. So the State of Virginia had Carrie sterilized against her will. When the Supreme Court upheld the sterilization law in *Buck v. Bell* in 1927, Justice Oliver Wendell Holmes, Jr., offered a succinct and chilling justification: "Three generations of imbeciles are enough."

A year later Carrie's sister Doris—who would no more be considered retarded by modern standards than her sister—was sterilized under the same law. When she was wheeled into the operating room to have her Fallopian tubes severed, Doris was told that the operation was to remove her appendix. Doris and her husband tried to have children throughout her childbearing years, and consulted doctors at three different hospitals. But no one could detect that she had been sterilized; the only evidence, after all, was the surgery scar, and Doris naturally told them that was from an unrelated operation. Doris Buck finally discovered in 1980—half a century after the Supreme Court decision that sealed her fate—that the Virginia eugenics law, and the highest court of justice in the land, were the cause of her tragically barren life.

The Court's cavalier acceptance of coercive sterilization of so-called mental defectives in *Buck v. Bell* is all the more frightening when one learns that the same tests and procedures that classified Carrie and Doris Buck as feebleminded indicated that fully one-half of the adult white males in America at that time were also "morons," with an average mental age of thirteen. (The tests also "revealed," as one might expect, that blacks, Mediterranean immigrants, and women were even more retarded.) Under such an expansive definition of feeblemindedness, few of us would be safe from the surgeon's knife.

When the Supreme Court next considered a sterilization law in 1942, it was less enthusiastic about granting society's majority the power to conduct biological experiments at the expense of the dignity and reproductive liberty of the minority. Oklahoma law provided for the sterilization of people convicted of two or more "felonies involving moral turpitude." This included such crimes as larceny, but expressly excluded embezzlement and tax fraud. The Court characterized the right to reproduce as "one of the basic civil rights of man" and noted that the statute's distinctions among crimes smacked of a particularly offensive class-based discrimination: lower-class chicken thieves were to be sterilized, but not upper-class felons who committed white-collar crimes. The Justices appear to have accorded reproductive freedom the status of a fundamental right in large part because of fear about the offensively selective and potentially genocidal way in which government control of reproduction might be exercised if the choice of whether or when to beget a child were to be transferred from the individual to the state.

Lest anyone be too quick to breathe a sigh of relief, it is worth noting that the Supreme Court has never actually repudiated its scandalous decision in *Buck v. Bell*. Indeed, the law upheld in that case was implemented for nearly half a century. By the time Virginia finally halted the program in 1972, more than seventy-five hundred people—most of them "unwed mothers, prostitutes, petty criminals or children with disciplinary problems"—had been sterilized by a government with its own peculiar plan for purifying the human race.

Government interference with individual reproductive autonomy has not been limited to preventing people from having children; indeed, most of the time the state has worked to *force* women to bear children, by denying them access to contraceptives and abortions. In 1923, although nearly every state had a law restricting the prescription and sale of contraceptives, only Connecticut absolutely banned the *use* of birth control devices. In February of that year the struggle to repeal this state assault on the most personal of rights began with the first public meeting of what would later become the Connecticut Planned Parenthood League. That meeting was organized by three prominent matrons—among them Katharine Houghton Hepburn, mother of the acclaimed actress. Hepburn was most incensed by the law's discriminatory impact: while wealthy women and their personal physicians could flout the law, the statute was highly effective in denying birth control to the poor or working-class women who needed it most. To the critics who labeled her an enemy of the family and a child hater, Mrs. Hepburn replied, "I have six children and I use birth control. If I didn't, I would have twenty-five children. You have to be sympathetic to the ones of us who are more fertile."

Despite the efforts of Hepburn and others, the birth control law was consistently upheld by the Connecticut courts and maintained by the legislature. It was still on the books in 1961, when Mrs. Estelle Griswold, a successor to Hepburn as leader of the Connecticut Planned Parenthood League, opened a birth control clinic in New Haven. Within three days the police were knocking on the door. Griswold was anxious to test the law in court, so she turned herself in, voluntarily closed the clinic, and asked several of the clinic's patients to serve as witnesses. When one of those women, the wife of a minister, was interviewed by the police, the detective took her birth control pills as evidence. She promptly called Griswold for a replacement prescription, saying, "I don't mind going to jail for this case, but getting pregnant would be something else."

In *Griswold v. Connecticut* in 1965 the Supreme Court declared the birth control law unconstitutional. In an echo of Justice Brandeis's emphasis on the "right to be let alone," the Court held that the decision of a woman and her husband to have children was within "a zone of privacy" protected from government intrusion. Justice William O. Douglas was most incensed by the only imaginable method of directly enforcing a ban on birth control. "Would we," he asked, "allow the police to search the sacred precincts of marital bedrooms for tell-tale signs of the use of contraceptives?" The seven Justices in the majority were undeterred by the fact that there is not a single word in the Constitution's text that proclaims a right of privacy, not even in general terms, let alone with respect to the "intimacies of the marital relationship." As Justice Douglas observed, "we deal with a right of privacy older than the Bill of Rights." But two Justices dissented; and many who might have been on the Court with them, or who might yet be nominated to sit as Justices, would make their dissenting view the law of the land.

In its 1972 decision in *Eisenstadt v. Baird*, the Supreme Court extended to unmarried persons the privacy right it had announced in *Griswold*. Justice Brennan wrote for the Court that "if the right of privacy means anything, it is the right of the *individual*, married or single, to be free from unwarranted governmental intrusion into matters so fundamentally affecting a person as the decision whether to bear or beget a child." But

Griswold's greatest impact was felt the following year, in the case of *Roe v. Wade.*

One summer evening in 1969 a twenty-five-year-old unmarried woman named Norma McCorvey was walking home from work along a country road. She was attacked by three men and two women, who gang-raped her and left her lying in the road. Her distress multiplied several weeks later when she discovered that she was pregnant. She could not bear the thought of giving birth to a child conceived of such an outrage, but abortion was illegal in Texas, and she lacked the resources to travel to New York or California. Although she was unable to terminate her own unwanted and involuntary pregnancy, McCorvey was willing to challenge the Texas abortion ban in court for the sake of other women. Her one condition, to protect her daughter by a previous marriage, was that she be anonymous; thus she was named in the lawsuit as Jane Roe. McCorvey had little education, and did not realize that her case might go to a very high court indeed. When her lawyer informed McCorvey that her case was to be presented to the Supreme Court of the United States, she was dismayed: "My God, all those people are so important. They don't have time to listen to some little old Texas girl who got in trouble."

But the Court did listen, and it invoked the right of privacy to secure for women a greater measure of reproductive autonomy—including a limited right to terminate a pregnancy. Right or wrong, the decision in *Roe v. Wade* fueled, rather than extinguished, the abortion controversy. As the mass bombings of family planning clinics in the early and mid-1980s demonstrated, the abortion issue remains violently divisive. Regardless of where one stands on the controversy, the Supreme Court's preeminent role is undeniable.

Moore v. City of East Cleveland shows how liberties that we take for granted can in fact be highly contingent—a change in a single Justice's vote could have thrown Mrs. Moore into jail and thrown her grandson out of her home. *Griswold* and *Roe* demonstrate that recognition of even our most personal and important

rights is not inevitable. The right of reproductive autonomy vindicated in those cases is expressed nowhere in
the Constitution's text—only in the vision of the seven
figures in black robes who voted to invalidate the birth
control and abortion bans as violations of "due process
of law." Because Justice Potter Stewart, having joined
the *Roe* majority, retired and was replaced in 1981 by
Justice Sandra Day O'Connor, the vote tally has changed.
The 1973 *Roe* decision was reaffirmed by the Court a
decade later in *City of Akron v. Akron Center for
Reproductive Health, Inc.*, but only by a vote of 6 to 3.
Future votes could be closer still, or could go the other
way altogether. This prospect should remind us that we
all have a very great stake in the choice of who is
appointed to the Supreme Court.

TECHNOLOGY, LIFE, AND DEATH

When advances in technology create new opportunities
for our lives, they also create new questions for the
Supreme Court. The authors of the Fourth Amendment
created a search warrant requirement to protect citizens from seizure of their personal papers and from
physical invasions of their homes. All they knew of
electricity was that Ben Franklin had flown his kites
during thunderstorms; they knew nothing of electronic
eavesdropping. The invention of the telephone created
a new form of private communication and the advent of
wiretapping provided a new way to violate privacy. The
Supreme Court thus had to decide what the Constitution says about this new phenomenon.

The challenges to the law posed by new technology
are most difficult where the advance engenders a clash
of powerful conflicting rights. The law banning abortion
in *Roe v. Wade* came to be seen as a constitutional
controversy only when medical technology made the
procedure safe for the mother. The Texas statute had
been enacted in 1854 to protect women from an operation that resulted not only in the destruction of the
fetus but also in the deaths of half of the pregnant

women who underwent it. The conflict of the mother's right of reproductive autonomy with the unborn child's right to live became an issue of law only when advances in the medical arts made abortion a generally realistic alternative to carrying a pregnancy to term. At the same time, the more people have learned about the fetus as a growing being with brain waves and familiar human features, the stronger have been the feelings of many that the woman's freedom is pitted against a genuine baby's life. The resolution of that conflict is not an easy task, no matter where one takes a stand, for both the fetus *and* the woman have claims to be protected from the whims of laws that unduly discount their interests.

The Supreme Court is not always eager to confront such tough problems. The birth control statute struck down in *Griswold v. Connecticut* had been presented to the Court in a different case several years before *Griswold* arose. At that time a majority of the Justices preferred to duck the issue and leave it for another day. But when *competing* claims of fundamental right are at stake, such ostrich maneuvers can at best conceal the fact that *anything* the Court does, including nothing at all, results in the securing of some asserted rights and the sacrifice of others. In such situations, allowing a challenged law to stand is itself a decision in favor of the status quo. For example, if the Supreme Court had refused to hear *Roe* at all, it would have effectively delegated the fate of mother and unborn child alike to shifting political majorities in the fifty state legislatures. The visible credit or blame for the outcome in each state might seem to rest with one or another legislative assembly. But ultimate responsibility for placing the choice *there* rather than with the women involved, or with guardians for the unborn, would still rest with the Supreme Court. Thus a posture of judicial restraint by the Court, far from consistently protecting *either* set of rights, would leave women unprotected in some states, the unborn defenseless in others.

So, too, if the Supreme Court ties its understanding of the Constitution's commands to technology instead of politics, it may build obsolescence into the law in a manner that has the *look* of inevitability but that traces, in the end, to decisions the Justices themselves have made. *Roe v. Wade* may already have been affected in this way. The right to terminate a pregnancy that was recognized in that case was made to turn on the ability of the fetus to survive outside the womb—the fetus's so-called viability. Under the *Roe* decision, as the fetus grows, the woman's reproductive autonomy diminishes while the state's power to regulate abortion expands. Once the fetus is medically viable, the state may ban abortion altogether so long as the mother's health is not endangered. In the decade between the decision in *Roe* in 1973 and its reaffirmation by the Court in three cases in 1983, the point of viability was pushed several weeks earlier into the gestation period by improved techniques of caring for premature infants. Artificial wombs may be available sooner than we think. Should the states then be allowed to outlaw abortion altogether in favor of a compulsory transfer from a human to a mechanical incubator? For better or worse, decisions like that will be in the Justices' hands. However much the Court's rulings may *seem* to make outcomes follow from scientific facts or technical necessities, it will be the Court that, in the background, shapes the lives we lead.

Other innovations in reproductive technology have already raised troubling questions. May a state impose responsibility for a child conceived by artificial insemination on the man who made the donation to a sperm bank? If such a child develops a hereditary disease, does it violate the donor's privacy if the state requires the sperm bank to reveal his identity to the parents and physicians of the child? Must a surrogate mother assume responsibility for her baby if those who contracted for the child decide not to accept it? And if a surrogate mother refuses to give up her baby as promised, are her maternal rights violated if the state steps in to snatch the infant from her embrace?

Innovations in medical technology create a host of new avenues for government intervention in our lives.

Today 80 percent of the Americans who die every year do so not at home or while at work but in a hospital. More and more of those individuals spend their final days trapped in the demeaning tangle of technology that has become death's least human face. A claim to meet one's end with dignity in the quiet of one's home carries great force. But what about a patient's demand to hasten his death? Death is still inevitable, but modern medicine gives us great powers to determine its timing. Since nature no longer makes the decision for us, we are left with a multitude of choices that implicate fundamental rights. And in our system the Supreme Court sets the ground rules by which those choices are made.

If your child is born with a congenital defect that threatens its life, are you free to refuse treatment that will save the infant but doom it to a tragically limited life? Or may the state compel you to authorize the life-saving procedure? In *Jehovah's Witnesses v. King County Hospital* in 1968 the Supreme Court upheld a state law that permitted children to be declared wards of the court in the event that their parents oppose blood transfusions for them, even if the family members are Jehovah's Witnesses, for whom a transfusion is a violation of divine law. But what if the medical treatment needed to save the child involves a great deal of risk and pain for the patient? Can a state force parents to endure the suffering of their child when the prospects for *any* kind of life, let alone a full one, are far from certain? Does the government violate the privacy of the parents by requiring the hospital to turn over its records so that the state may judge for itself whether the parents and doctors have made the "right" decision?

Should the answer to any of these questions be different if we deal not with a newborn child but with an adult, who simply prefers to forgo heroic efforts to prolong his misery? And if the adult is to have the right to refuse treatment, how do we justify denying that same choice to a child or a comatose patient? Does a state law allowing someone to turn off a coma victim's life support system deprive that patient of life without due process of law? If not, *who* should be competent to choose between life and death for those not competent to make the decision themselves? Should the family have unfettered discretion to unplug a comatose relative's iron lung or discontinue intravenous feeding? Should a judge be involved? Or should the decision be put by the Supreme Court into the hands of the "experts" —the physicians and the hospital ethics committee?

The problems posed by medical technology are not only matters of privacy and autonomy; there is also the question of allocating scarce resources—dividing up too few things among too many claimants. The number of artificial hearts, kidney dialysis machines, and human organs available for transplants is limited. Who is to have priority in access to such lifesaving wonders? May a state create a free market, and allow the coveted commodity to go to the highest bidder? Would laws allowing hospitals to favor children over senior citizens in the distribution of transplants or scarce machines deny the older patients the equal protection of the laws?

A society such as ours must ultimately answer these questions with laws. And given the vital and momentous rights involved, the Constitution itself will inevitably come into play. Therefore the Supreme Court, as the final arbiter of the Constitution's meaning, cannot long avoid these issues. Repose is not the destiny of the Court, and it will eventually be called upon to help make the choices thrust upon us by science. For the Barney Clarks, the Karen Quinlans, the Baby Faes, and the Baby Jane Does—the animal and artificial hearts and lungs, the heroically saved infants and the brain-dead adults—will be with us no matter what the Justices decide. But what the Justices decide will set the terms in which the full range of life and death decisions will in turn be made.

THE FATE OF MINORITIES

Even when the Congress and the President can be counted upon to defend most of us from the infringement of fundamental liberties, because the political majorities to which those departments of government answer demand such protection, the Supreme Court often stands alone as the guardian of minority groups. The democratic political process, by its very nature, leaves political minorities vulnerable to the will of the majority. True, the Supreme Court's record in championing the cause of oppressed minorities is hardly unstained. The decision in 'Dred Scott v. Sandford in 1857, which relegated black Americans to the status of property, and the Korematsu case in 1944, which upheld the internment of Japanese Americans, mark the depths to which the Court has occasionally sunk. Yet in the series of race discrimination cases in the 1950s and '60s that followed the landmark 1954 decision in Brown v. Board of Education, the Supreme Court made historic strides in bringing to fulfillment the Fourteenth Amendment's promise of equality before the law. Other cases have begun to do the same on behalf of resident aliens, illegitimate children, and the physically and mentally handicapped.

The Court has also been called upon to ensure the liberties of women, who lack political power proportional to their numbers and thus often function as a "minority," despite their demographic status as a majority. In the last fifteen years, the Supreme Court has repeatedly struck down legislative efforts to enact into law sexist stereotypes about the "weaker sex." Implicit in the Court's sex discrimination cases is a recognition that women are denied the equal protection of the laws by statutes and ordinances that arbitrarily freeze biological differences into social and economic destiny. In 1974, for example, in Cleveland Board of Education v. LaFleur, the Court struck down mandatory maternity leave policies that required all schoolteachers to stop teaching after the fourth month of pregnancy. Naturally, only women were put at a disadvantage by the law. The Court declared that such policies imposed an unconstitutional burden on women's exercise of the fundamental "freedom of personal choice in matters of marriage and family life." Whenever it enters the arena on behalf of racial and religious minorities, or on behalf of other relatively powerless groups, the Supreme Court does nothing more than make good on the promise of the Constitution that certain crucial liberties will be forever protected from the vicissitudes of the political process.

In the *LaFleur* case and many of the others discussed here, the Supreme Court based its decisions on the Constitution. The Court also plays an influential role in our lives when it interprets and applies the laws written by Congress. When the Court reads federal statutes generously, be they consumer protection laws or civil rights measures, Congress's power to protect our rights and enhance the quality of our lives is at its fullest. On the other hand, when the Court hands down a narrow or just plain incorrect interpretation of a statute, Congress's efforts are stymied. Sometimes Congress can pass a new law that effectively overturns the Court's ruling; statutory—unlike constitutional—decisions, can be reversed by new legislation, and do not require an amendment to the Constitution. For example, in *General Electric Company v. Gilbert* in 1976, the Supreme Court held that an employer's health insurance plan that paid benefits for nonoccupational illness and accidents, but not for absence due to pregnancy, did not violate the Civil Rights Act because it did not discriminate between men and women, but discriminated only between pregnant and nonpregnant persons. Two years later Congress passed the pregnancy Discrimination Act, effectively telling the Supreme Court that it had made a glaring mistake—that, although not all women are pregnant persons, all pregnant persons are women, and therefore the distinction is obviously discriminatory and should be deemed unlawful.

But sometimes the Congress finds the Supreme Court's statutory misinterpretations more difficult to overturn. In the case of *Grove City College v. Bell* the Court in

1984 held that another section of the Civil Rights Act did not require a cutoff of all federal funds to a college that refused to demonstrate its compliance with the laws banning sex discrimination; only those programs directly receiving the federal funds had to comply with the law. Despite broad agreement among the members of Congress that the Court had once again misread the statute, immediate efforts to pass a new law stumbled over the tangled political threads of the legislative process. As Congress adjourned in 1984 a small minority of the Senate had made it impossible, at least in the short run, to undo the mischief wrought by the Supreme Court in the *Grove City* case.

PRESERVING DEMOCRACY

Part of the Supreme Court's institutional sensitivity to the rights of minorities stems from the fact that the political process tends to discount and overlook them. Since the late 1940s the Court has taken on a major role in preserving the democratic process not just on behalf of minorities but on behalf of the entire electorate by rooting out legislative malapportionment. In such historic cases as *Baker v. Carr* and *Reynolds v. Sims* in the 1960s, the Supreme Court plunged headlong into the political thicket to give life to the principle of "one person, one vote." The Court ordered that the boundaries of state and congressional electoral districts be redrawn along population lines, so that the political voices of some voters would not be muffled by their submersion in overcrowded constituencies, while the voices of other voters in less populous districts were amplified.

When we cast our ballots today in a congressional or state legislative race, one vote "counts" as much as any other only because the Supreme Court has said that it must; nothing in the Constitution's text specifies that result in so many words—although the Constitution's preamble, in its reference to "We the People," and the Fourteenth Amendment, in its reference to "equal protection of the laws," are obviously suggestive. And we exercise our franchise in all state elections without first having to pay a poll tax only because the Court has determined that states may not, as a matter of equal protection, distribute the right to vote on the basis of ability to pay; nothing in the Constitution expressly prohibits that practice, although the Twenty-fourth Amendment, ratified in 1964, forbids poll taxes in federal elections. These protections are typical of the ways in which the Supreme Court has sought to guarantee each of us an equal say in how we are governed.

FEDERALISM: THE STATES, THE NATION, AND THE ECONOMY

Two things have held this nation together for the last two centuries: the insistence of visionaries like Abraham Lincoln that the states may not secede from the Union, and the Framers' insight that the most glaring failure of the Articles of Confederation was their inability to control interstate economic warfare. The former was finally resolved by the Civil War; the latter by the Constitution's Commerce Clause. But in overcoming the internecine skirmishing of the states, the Framers needed both the Congress and the Supreme Court; the Commerce Clause was but the seed to the solution.

Chief Justice Marshall nurtured that seed in 1819 in *McCulloch v. Maryland*. The State of Maryland had attacked the Bank of the United States by attempting to levy a tax on its local branch. The Chief Justice denounced the tax and coined the adage "The power to tax is the power to destroy," thereby upholding Congress's power to create a national bank secure from state assault as a "necessary and proper" way to carry into effect laws "on which the welfare of a nation essentially depends." The *Bank Cases*, such as *McCulloch*, involved the major political controversy of the age and were therefore a fitting stage for the unfolding of the drama of the Commerce Clause. Yet the true potential of that clause was not revealed until Aaron Ogden sued his former business partner Thomas Gibbons for operating a steamboat ferry between New York and New Jersey in violation of the monopoly Ogden held from New York's legislature. Chief Justice Marshall's 1824 opinion for the Court in *Gibbons v. Ogden* struck down New York's power to grant Ogden or anyone else such a monopoly because it conflicted with the federal licensing scheme under which Gibbons was authorized to engage in interstate navigation. The Chief Justice wrote that the constitutional delegation to Congress of the authority "to regulate Commerce among the several states" extended that body's "plenary" authority to *all* activity having *any* interstate impact, however indirect.

A century later, in the 1935 case of *Baldwin v. Seelig*, the Supreme Court reaffirmed the Constitution's plan to outlaw parochial favoritism and interstate economic reprisals not only by delegating broad commerce power to Congress, but also by banning any acts of state protectionism that are not congressionally authorized. Justice Cardozo wrote that "the Constitution was framed upon the theory that the peoples of the several states must sink or swim together, and that in the long run prosperity and salvation are in union and not division." Such words have had a profound effect on our national history, but their impact in individual cases has been especially telling: bereft of his steamboat monopoly, Aaron Ogden went bankrupt, while Thomas Gibbons died a millionaire.

In a series of cases in the 1930s and 1940s, such as *NLRB v. Jones & Laughlin Steel Corp.*, the Supreme Court reversed a previous forty-year trend and once again endorsed an expansive reading of Congress's power to regulate interstate commerce. When it finally upheld President Roosevelt's New Deal legislation in such cases as *United States v. Darby* in 1941, the Court approved a sweeping redistribution of power from the states to the federal government.

The actual words of the Commerce Clause are few, but the Supreme Court has found in them a delegation to Congress of the power to protect the nation's "stream of commerce" from the ravages of private industrial warfare among labor unions and corporations, and to guarantee to workers who toil anywhere near the banks of that expansive waterway a reasonable wage, as well as freedom from unfair or discriminatory working conditions. As a result of Supreme Court decisions over the last half century, the federal government has a powerful voice in deciding the size of your paycheck, the benefits of your pension plan, the structure of your union and the safety of your workplace.

Under the guidance of the Court, the emphasis in the name "United States" has gradually but steadily shifted from "States" to "United." Our notion of "federalism" has changed from the glue that binds the states together to a universal solvent in which the boundaries of the states have become far less distinct. In 1978 the Court held that Alaska may not discriminate against those from out of state by imposing an obligation on the employers who operate the state's booming oil industry to hire Alaskans first. Four years later the Court struck down Alaska's plan for sharing with its citizens the embarrassment of riches that flowed from oil fields at Prudhoe Bay. The state decided to reward those who had been loyal residents even before the oil boom, so the size of the dividend received from the state treasury was based on years of residence—old-timers got fatter checks than recent arrivals. The Court declared the scheme unconstitutional, because it discriminated against those who moved into Alaska from other states and created degrees of citizenship on the basis of length of residence. Laws that place a disadvantage on new residents inhibit our freedom to travel among the fifty states. In this way, the Court protects our equal citizenship in "one Nation indivisible."

On the other hand, the Court has vindicated the right of cities and states to give preference to their own citizens in access to opportunities and goods created solely by voluntary local efforts and expenditures, such as public construction jobs. And a state university may provide admissions preferences and tuition breaks to state residents. Nor has the federal commerce power completely overwhelmed the states. The Supreme Court has allowed the states to engage in important economic regulation when it has perceived gaps in Congress's extensive network of legislation. For example, in *Pacific Gas & Electric Company v. California Energy Commission*, the Court held in 1983 that Congress has not totally preempted the field of nuclear energy regulation, but has left to the states the freedom to decide for themselves, on economic grounds, the future of nuclear power within their borders. Thus has the Supreme Court recognized the virtue of diversity. As Justice Brandeis observed in 1932, "it is one of the happy incidents of the federal system that a single courageous state may, if its citizens choose, serve as a laboratory; and try novel social and economic experiments without risk to the rest of the country." When the Supreme Court allows the states latitude to create jobs for their citizens, to choose different energy destinies, and to design their own unique programs of land-use zoning, taxation, and social services, it preserves for us all a breadth of possibilities.

WAR AND PEACE

Few issues of government are fraught with greater moment than the way a nation goes to war. Perhaps because questions of foreign policy are generally thought to be inappropriate for judicial resolution, the Supreme Court's influence on how our country makes war has been exerted largely by acquiescence. In the *Prize Cases* of 1863 the Court endorsed President Lincoln's decision to commit the nation to war without a formal declaration of hostilities by Congress, which opponents argued was required by the Constitution. When invasion or rebellion threatens, the Court declared, the President, as Commander in Chief, must be free to meet the war "as it presents itself, without waiting for Congress to baptize it with a name." In this century the Supreme Court sanctioned by default the President's authority to wage the Vietnam War: it refused to hear cases brought by draftees and lawmakers who challenged that executive power.

But the Supreme Court has apparently felt itself to be on its own turf when it comes to presidential arrogations of *domestic* authority during times of war, and has thus been more assertive in that domain. In 1866 the Court struck down the imposition of martial law in Indiana during the Civil War in *Ex parte Milligan*. The Court declared that since there were no hostilities in Indiana and the federal courts were open and operating, the military courts-martial had no jurisdiction to try civilians. In *Duncan v. Kahanamoku* in 1946, the Supreme Court reached the same decision with respect to martial rule established in Hawaii in the wake of the attack on Pearl Harbor. It is fair to ask whether the Court's resolve would have been so firm had it decided these cases while the wars in question were still being fought. Perhaps not: recall its shamefully disappointing performance in *Korematsu v. United States*. The Supreme Court, in that time of xenophobic hysteria, held that a gross violation of the Bill of Rights was justified by the military judgment that some of the imprisoned American citizens of Japanese ancestry might be disloyal to the United States.

The authorities in charge of that roundup of Asian Americans offered the Orwellian justification that the absence of actual *instances* of disloyalty was itself suspicious: it was said that only a sinister conspiracy could account for the uniformly exemplary behavior of those whose Japanese ancestry surely made them sympathetic to the enemy. Fred Korematsu's conviction for failure to report to a "relocation camp" was finally, if belatedly, vacated in 1983 by a federal district court. When Korematsu and 110,000 other Americans were robbed of most of their property and herded into concentration camps, the majestic language of the Constitution assured them that they could not be deprived of their property or liberty without "due process of law," and that they would always receive the "equal protection of the laws." But the Court decided not to enforce those promises in time of war. Without a vigilant and resolute Supreme Court, our most precious liberties are only words on yellowed parchment.

WHAT AMERICA STANDS FOR

Even though the Supreme Court speaks only when deciding actual cases, its discourse is sometimes conducted at a higher level than that literally necessary for the resolution of the particular disputes in question. The Justices speak in resonant tones on themes that transcend the outcome of a given controversy, and go to the very heart of what we are as a nation. For this reason the Supreme Court has been called "the schoolmaster of the Republic."

Sometimes the Court's lesson seems directed at reminding us of what is most important to us as a people. In the 1964 case of *Wesberry v. Sanders* the Court testified to the fundamental character of the right to vote:

> No right is more precious in a free country than that of having a choice in the election of those who make the laws under which, as good citizens, they must live. Other rights, even the most basic, are illusory if the right to vote is undermined.

No less fundamental than the right to *take* part is the right to *stand apart*. Walter Barnette and his family were Jehovah's Witnesses, who believed that saluting the American flag was tantamount to giving homage to a graven image, and that was a sin. In 1941 the West Virginia State Board of Education required all students to begin the school day with the Pledge of Allegiance to the Flag. Children who refused were expelled; some were adjudged delinquent and sent to juvenile reformatories. The parents of such children were prosecuted and were liable to fines and imprisonment. When his children were expelled and he was indicted for contributing to their delinquency, Walter Barnette went to court. In *West Virginia Bd. of Education v. Barnette*, the Court upheld the right of schoolchildren to refuse, as a matter of conscience, to salute the flag. In words that have deservedly been quoted often, Justice Robert Jackson in 1943 reaffirmed the American dedication to freedom of thought:

> If there is any fixed star in our constitutional constellation, it is that no official, high or petty, can prescribe what shall be orthodox in politics, nationalism, religion, or other matters of opinion, or force citizens to confess by word or act their faith therein. If there are any circumstances which permit an exception, they do not now occur to us.

Contemporaneous events in 1943 may have influenced the Court's choice of words, for Nazi Germany must have presented a sobering lesson on the cost of enforcing compulsory and uniform patriotic zeal. Sixteen years earlier Justice Brandeis had explored the Constitution's commitment to freedom of opinion in words whose relevance has not diminished. "Those who won our independence believed that the final end of the state was to make men free to develop their faculties. . . . They valued liberty both as an end and as a means." The Supreme Court has staunchly upheld this "freedom to think as you will and to speak as you think" as a "means indispensable to the discovery and spread of political truth." Our forefathers believed, in Justice Brandeis's words, "that public discussion is a political duty; and that this should be a fundamental principle of the American government":

> They recognized the risks to which all human institutions are subject. But they knew that order cannot be secured merely through fear of punishment for its infraction; that it is hazardous to discourage thought, hope and imagination; that fear breeds repression; that repression breeds hate; that hate menaces stable government; that the path of safety lies in the oppor-

tunity to discuss freely supposed grievances and proposed remedies; and that the fitting remedy for evil counsels is good ones.

The Supreme Court's tutelage has extended beyond tolerance for different opinions to tolerance for different behavior. In 1957 Kenneth Donaldson was committed to a Florida state mental institution by his father because of the latter's belief that his son "was not quite right." Kenneth's frequent attempts to gain his release were blocked by the institution's superintendent, Dr. J. B. O'Connor. O'Connor admitted that his patient was no threat to himself or anyone else and that he was capable of taking care of himself, but the superintendent nevertheless kept Donaldson locked up because he considered him "mentally ill"; Donaldson received no therapy of any kind for his "illness" during the fifteen years of his confinement.

In his opinion for the Court in *O'Connor v. Donaldson* in 1975, Justice Potter Stewart directed our attention to the critical question:

> May the state fence in the harmlessly mentally ill solely to save its citizens from exposure to those whose ways are different? One might as well ask if the state, to avoid public unease, could incarcerate all who are physically unattractive or socially eccentric. Mere public intolerance or animosity cannot constitutionally justify the deprivation of a person's physical liberty.

So, too, society may not erect walls to keep out those whose color it finds objectionable. In the 1954 case of *Brown v. Board of Education*, the Court unanimously denounced racial segregation in the nation's schools. In so doing, the Justices breathed new life into the potentially sterile phrase "equal protection of the laws" and set a national agenda for racial justice. Separate schools for black and white children, the Court explained, could never be equal, for segregating black children "from others of similar age and qualifications solely because of their race generates a feeling of inferiority as to their status in the community that may affect their hearts and minds in a way unlikely ever to be undone." Such a demoralizing and debilitating system of racial apartheid had no place in the American vision; and therefore had to be eliminated "with all deliberate speed." The massive resistance to school integration that followed *Brown*, and the billboards erected in the South that called for the impeachment of Chief Justice Earl Warren, revealed that the teachings of the republic's schoolmaster are not always received by all its pupils with appreciation and admiration.

Nor have the lessons taught by the Supreme Court always been full of hope and promise for the liberties that we claim to cherish as a people. A century before its call for an end to racial segregation in *Brown v. Board of Education*, the Supreme Court had held in *Dred Scott v. Sandford* that blacks, whether enslaved or emancipated, could never be citizens because they were "not part of the American people." Chief Justice Taney, who eventually freed his own slaves, wrote in that infamous case that blacks were not people but property. They had come to what would later be called the land of opportunity not as immigrants but as "articles of merchandise."

Women, too, have not always received the Court's full respect. Mrs. Myra Bradwell had been judicially certified to be of "good character" and found on "due examination to possess the requisite qualifications" to be an attorney, but Illinois was not impressed. She took her case to the Supreme Court in 1873. But even though this was after the ratification of the Fourteenth Amendment to the Constitution, which guarantees to all Americans the privileges and immunities of national citizenship, and which promises all of a state's residents the equal protection of its laws, the Court held that women could be categorically barred by a state from the practice of law. In *Bradwell v. Illinois* Justice Joseph P. Bradley declared that the "idea of a woman adopting a distinct and independent career from that of her husband" is "repugnant," for the "paramount destiny and mission of woman are to fulfill the noble and benign offices of wife and mother. This is the law of the Creator." This was the teaching of the same Justice Bradley who, the very same year, had dissented in the *Slaughterhouse Cases* because of his conviction that "the right to choose one's calling is an essential part of liberty," and that, without the right to butcher sheep and slaughter pigs for pay, "one cannot be a freeman."

The Supreme Court no longer endorses such oppressive stereotypes of women, but the persistence in some quarters of Justice Bradley's opinions about women's proper place suggests that, whether progressive or retrograde, the teachings of the Court perpetuate as well as mirror the beliefs of the age. The Court's visions of society have telling consequences for all of us; even this brief survey of the terrain the Supreme Court has traversed over the past two centuries should leave no doubt that the Court matters deeply to us all, and that the question of who sits on the Court is therefore a matter of paramount national importance.

Chapter Two

WHAT DIFFERENCE CAN
A JUSTICE OR TWO MAKE?

The choice of Justices affects our lives not only when the Court is viewed as a collective whole but also when even a single vacancy or pair of vacancies is at stake. That stark reality is easy for many of us to forget. With the Constitution as their fulcrum, the nine Justices acting as a group sometimes seem almost able to move the Earth. But is it really true that just one or two Justices can make a massive difference? Consider the track record.

Despite the comment made by Justice Rehnquist in his 1984 Court-packing speech, Justices do not always come to the Court "one at a time." But there remains the fundamental assertion behind the "one at a time" idea: each individual Justice, or even a pair of new members, is said to be swallowed up by the institution of the Court, and is therefore not in a position to reshape its course. Alternatively, as Justice Rehnquist also suggested in the same speech, the Court's "centrifugal forces" can be perceived as so powerful that the Justices may be expected to grow completely independent of one another, each becoming an island unreachable by any "hierarchical order" or "institutional unity." The argument is that because the Justices are appointed for life and answer only to their own conscience, they are less concerned with being "team players" and more concerned with securing their individual places in history.

In different ways, these seemingly contradictory images serve to make the same point by denying the idea that one or two Justices can make a major difference at the Court. But to the extent that they share a grain of truth, both observations leave the door open to many ways in which just one or two Justices *can* make a difference, and a crucial one.

THE FIVE-TO-FOUR COURT

Even those who accept the idea of "centrifugal forces" on the Court would have to acknowledge the difference that one Justice can make when the Court is closely divided and renders a 5–4 decision. Such decisions are far more common than some might suppose. About one-fifth of the Court's cases in the decade from 1974 to 1984 were decided on a 5–4 basis. Yet this is a Court not known for ideological divisions or intramural rivalries as sharp and deep as some previous Courts have experienced. If it seems surprising or unsettling that so large a fraction of the constitutional choices made in the 1970s and 1980s have turned on the narrowest of margins, there is some comfort in learning that the phenomenon is hardly a new one. For one Justice to make the difference in critical Supreme Court rulings about the country's course is a tradition that dates back to the early nineteenth century. Some of the Court's early decisions to grant states broad power to modify their own contracts (the 1837 *Charles River Bridge* case), to draw limits on state power to tax immigrants (the 1849 *Passenger Cases*), or to impose restraints on state ability to issue bills of credit (*Craig v. Missouri*, decided in 1830) were resolved by margins of one Justice. The great Civil War cases testing the boundaries of presidential and national power (the *Prize Cases* and the *Test Oath Cases*) were all decided by Courts split 5 to 4. Later decisions to hold the use of greenbacks as "legal tender" unconstitutional in 1870 (in *Hepburn v. Griswold*), and then constitutional the very next year (in *Knox v. Lee*), turned on the difference of one Justice's vote. The famous *Slaughterhouse Cases* of 1873, which were the first major attempts to interpret the Fourteenth Amendment, were 5–4 rulings.

Nearer to the turn of the century and in the early 1900s, the Court's string of conservative economic rulings were often handed down in 5–4 decisions. For example, the 1895 decision to hold the income tax unconstitutional in *Pollock v. Farmers Loan and Trust Co.*, the 1905 decision to strike down a New York maximum hours law for laborers in *Lochner v. New York*, and the 1918 ruling that invalidated a federal child labor statute in *Hammer v. Dagenhart*, were all 5 to 4. And many of the Court's famous New Deal rulings likewise turned on 5–4 votes. For example, the Court's early 1930s concessions to the New Deal—upholding a Minnesota mortgage moratorium in *Home Building & Loan v. Blaisdell*, sustaining a New York price control on milk in *Nebbia v. New York*, and upholding Congress's repudiation of the gold standard in the *Gold Clause Cases*—each turned on the vote of a single Justice. When the Court then struck out at the New Deal in 1935 and 1936, it invalidated the Railroad Retirement Act and a New York minimum wage law by a single-vote margin. Finally, when the famous 1937 turnabout occurred, the Court, by similar 5–4 votes, sustained a Washington minimum wage law in *West Coast Hotel v. Parrish* and the National Labor Relations Act in *NLRB v. Jones & Laughlin Steel Corp.*

Many of the post–World War II loyalty and security decisions, which sustained loyalty oath requirements and anti-Communist statutes, were decided by 5–4 margins. And the landmark criminal defense rulings of the early 1960s—requiring the exclusion by state courts of illegally obtained evidence in *Mapp v. Ohio*, extending the Fifth Amendment privilege against compelled self-incrimination to state proceedings in *Malloy v. Hogan*, and guaranteeing a suspect's right to counsel during interrogation in *Escobedo v. Illinois*—all depended on the vote of one Justice. The famous 1966 ruling in *Miranda v. Arizona* that suspects must be informed of their rights when subjected to "custodial interrogation" was one of the Court's most important 5–4 decisions. And, by 5–4 votes, the Court has more recently cut back on many of these very protections. The Court's landmark 1972 decision in *Furman v. Georgia*, striking down all death penalty statutes as then administered, was 5–4, as was its 1976 holding in *Woodson v. North Carolina* that new death penalty laws could not make capital punishment mandatory for any particular class of crimes.

The 5–4 decisions run the gamut of issues, and show no sign of disappearing. In 1972 the Court upheld a sweeping program of secret government surveillance of peaceful civil rights and civil liberties meetings, refusing by a 5–4 vote to allow any First Amendment challenge to the program to be brought by the individuals being spied upon. (In that case, the fifth vote for the majority was cast by Justice Rehnquist, who refused to disqualify himself despite his recent role as a Justice Department lawyer defending the contested surveillance activity.) In 1978 the Court addressed the subject of affirmative action in its 5–4 decision upholding some affirmative action programs but barring the use of numerical "quotas" to aid minority students in *University of California v. Bakke*. In 1984 alone, the Court ruled by the narrowest of margins in favor of the constitutionality of city-sponsored nativity scenes in *Lynch v. Donnelly*, the legality of home videotape recording in *Sony Corp. of America v. Universal City Studios*, and the President's power to ban travel to Cuba in *Regan v. Wald*. These examples only begin to illustrate the scope and importance such close decisions can have.

Key 5–4 decisions are thus more than a century old, and will be with us as long as the Court is. They serve as reminders that one Justice can, and does, make a difference in the choice among possible constitutional futures.

FORECASTING THE PAST

Over the course of a long judicial career, one Justice's voting pattern might differ strikingly from that of another. Only if we know who might have been appointed in a Justice's place can we say with confidence how decisively a given appointment really affected ultimate results.

But how do we forecast the past? After all, there is usually no way to know which person would have been nominated for a seat on the Court if the person ultimately selected had been passed over. Yet in cases where the Senate has rejected one nominee and confirmed instead a subsequent choice, we do have tangible evidence of just how great a difference one Justice can make.

No case demonstrates that difference more dramatically than the substitution of Owen Roberts for John Parker on the Court. Parker, a forty-five-year-old federal judge from North Carolina with a reputation for antilabor, conservative decisions, was rejected by a narrow 41–39 Senate confirmation vote in 1930. In his place, President Hoover nominated the more moderate fifty-five-year-old Pennsylvanian Owen Roberts. Roberts became the Justice who switched his vote on minimum wage laws in 1937, abandoning the Court's conservative "Four Horsemen" on the validity of state economic regulation and joining four other Justices to begin upholding key elements of the New Deal package at the federal level.

Roberts's switch was critical in sidetracking President Franklin Roosevelt's controversial "Court-packing" bill, an attempt to add six new Justices to the Court and ensure its support of the Roosevelt program. Had Parker been on the Court, would he have switched as Roberts did? If not, would the Court-packing bill have passed? If it had, what then?

To take another, more recent case, there is the Senate's 1970 rejection of former segregationist G. Harrold Carswell, and the subsequent approval of Nixon nominee Harry Blackmun to the Court. Justice Blackmun has been quite liberal on racial issues coming before the Court and has been a key figure in the Court's development of pro-choice principles in the abortion area. Would Carswell have played a parallel role? We are entitled to doubt it.

THE "CRITICAL MASS" THEORY

Often the Court rests on a delicate balance between two blocks of Justices split on some issue, with one or more others positioned between the rival camps. In such a case, the addition of one Justice to the Court can serve to create a "critical mass" of Justices that tips the Court firmly to one side, eventually bringing others along as well.

The appointment of Senator Hugo Black by F.D.R. took the delicately balanced Court of four New Deal opponents, three supporters, and two Justices in the middle (Owen Roberts and Charles Evan Hughes) and turned it into a Court willing to give solid support to F.D.R.'s initiatives. So, too, Arthur Goldberg's appointment to the Court in 1962 shifted a tenuous balance on matters of personal liberty toward a consistent libertarianism, assuring Chief Justice Warren and Justices Black, Douglas, and Brennan a solid majority for their views on civil liberties issues.

Any Court as delicately balanced as that of the 1980s is capable of being thrown squarely to one side of the ideological divide by an appointment that upsets still narrow margins on key questions.

CATALYSTS ON THE COURT

Beyond the potentially pivotal role of the Justice's own vote, a Justice's persuasive powers may often make a difference by rallying colleagues. The difference in these cases may go well beyond simply changing a result or a margin of victory; a "catalytic" Justice may even be able to change the Court's very chemistry, altering its understanding of the basis of its decisions, and therefore changing the development of the constitutional law the Court announces. Such a Justice can also play a key role in the separation of the hundred-odd cases the Court chooses to hear annually from the many thousands it turns away.

For example, in the Court's internal discussion of

Grosjean v. American Press Co., Inc.—a 1936 case involving a Louisiana law that taxed the receipts of certain newspapers in the state (those which opposed Governor Huey Long)—it was unanimously agreed that the law would be struck down, but there was dispute over what the basis of the decision would be. Justice Sutherland carried the day for the more conservative Justices on the Court, and won an agreement that the decision would rest on the state's discrimination against certain commercial enterprises under the Fourteenth Amendment's Equal Protection Clause. But Justice Cardozo drafted an alternate opinion resting the decision on a far more novel ground: application of the First Amendment to prohibit state—instead of simply federal— laws hindering freedom of the press. Cardozo's opinion proved so powerful that Justice Sutherland adopted it in place of his original draft of the Court's official ruling. The landmark holding in that case, especially coming from the pen of a Justice—George Sutherland—known for his conservative opinions, was a major advance in the law of the First Amendment. In 1931 only five Justices had been willing to apply the First Amendment to state laws; a unanimous Court did so in 1936 as a result of Cardozo's intervention.

Justice Brennan played a similar catalytic role in many of the difficult and often pathbreaking cases decided by the Warren Court. He organized his brethren and articulated the Court's broader vision of the Constitution in *Baker v. Carr*, when the Court held that it could rule on the validity of a state legislature's apportionment, and in the 1964 case of *New York Times v. Sullivan*, which limited the ability of public officials to bring libel actions against the press. Catalytic Justices, another established tradition on the Court, prove that one Justice can often make much more than one vote's difference. One person's persuasive judicial skills are often the key to taking the Court to new frontiers of constitutional law.

STAKING OUT THE GROUND

One Justice can also make the difference in the important, if difficult to document role of broadening the range of acceptable views on the Court or redefining the "center" by staking out the ground at one end of the ideological spectrum. Justice William O. Douglas's persistent liberal rulings in many criminal defense and civil liberties cases widened the scope of options seriously considered by the Court, and may have allowed more liberal views to seem distinctly "moderate." In the other direction, the addition of Justice Rehnquist's conservative ideology to the Court has "staked out the right" for a more moderate majority, and allowed Chief Justice Warren Burger to lead the Court toward—if not to—the Rehnquist perspective.

Like the "rabbit" technique often used by track teams—the tactic in which one competitor keeps up the pace by running far in front of the field, knowing that he cannot win but simply hoping to aid a comrade in gaining victory—a justice who trailblazes an ideological outlook on the Court normally will not carry the day. But his legacy can influence an entire era.

THE CHIEFS

The Chief Justices—only fifteen have served in our entire history—present the most obvious examples of the "one Justice who can make a difference." Although often in dissent, and sometimes lagging behind instead of leading the Court, one Chief may make all the difference in the constitutional world. No example better proves this point than Chief Justice John Marshall. The legendary Chief Justice personally wrote the opinion of the Court in 519 of the 1,215 cases decided during his tenure on the Court. Of the decisions that involved interpretation of the Constitution, Marshall penned the Court's judgment in more than half. Marshall was able to keep his Federalist majority together for dozens of key decisions, absorbing appointments by Democratic

Republican Presidents Jefferson, Madison, and Monroe. His intellectual grip on his fellow Justices was so firm that Marshall dissented from a constitutional ruling only once: in every other major case decided in his thirty-four years at the helm of the Supreme Court, Marshall got his way.

In the twentieth century the changing of the Chiefs has translated into an important difference in the Court's direction. For example, most observers believed that Chief Justice Fred Vinson was ambivalent about the constitutionality of school segregation, and uncertain about what position he would take after hearing arguments in a series of cases in 1953. Instead of deciding the cases, the Court ordered their reargument the following year. In the interim, Vinson died and a new Chief Justice, Earl Warren, took his place. The new Chief not only wrote the Court's precedent-shattering decision in *Brown v. Board of Education*, signaling the end of segregated public schools in this country, but also worked with his Associate Justices to develop an opinion that could be announced unanimously. That the Court spoke with a single, authoritative voice in *Brown* added immeasurably to the ruling's credibility in the face of widespread and bitter resistance.

The difference that seemingly unrelated events can make in the fate of a Chief Justice and of the Court is dramatically evident in the case of Justice Arthur Goldberg. When President Lyndon Johnson asked Goldberg to leave the Court in 1965 to help Johnson resolve the Vietnam conflict as ambassador to the United Nations, no one could have imagined the way the judicial dominoes would subsequently fall. Johnson chose his old friend Abe Fortas to replace Justice Goldberg, and thereby set off a chain of events that certainly changed the course of judicial history. When Chief Justice Earl Warren retired in 1968, Johnson nominated then Justice Fortas to replace him. Fortas failed to win confirmation for a variety of reasons relating to his service on the Court—a service made possible only because of Justice Goldberg's resignation. Fortas's critics pointed to his liberal opinions while a Justice, his continuing practice of advising Johnson on policy matters, and his acceptance of privately raised funds to teach a law school course while on the Court. Furthermore, to replace Fortas as an Associate Justice, Johnson named his Texas friend Homer Thornberry, adding fuel to the charges of "cronyism" that Fortas himself had to face.

All of this happened only because Arthur Goldberg had left the Supreme Court. What would have happened if he had remained? Among other things, it is entirely conceivable that Abe Fortas, if nominated to the Chief Justice's position directly from his private law practice, would have escaped the criticism that prevented his elevation from his position on the Court to its center seat. Or perhaps someone other than Fortas—someone who would have been confirmed—would have been nominated by President Johnson. In either case, someone other than Warren Burger would have served as Chief Justice from the late 1960s through the mid 1980s or beyond.

THE COURT'S FIRST FEMALE JUSTICE

Justice Goldberg can hardly be faulted for anticipating none of this when he decided to resign. Nor can Justice Potter Stewart be credited or blamed for the quite different votes cast by his successor, Justice Sandra Day O'Connor, in the wake of his 1981 resignation from the Court at the judicially youthful age of sixty-six. But the consequences of this single change on the Court demonstrate anew how a one-Justice switch can shift the direction of the entire Court.

On some issues, of course, there is no reason to believe that Justice O'Connor's votes differ from those that Justice Stewart would have cast. Taken as a whole, however, there are sharp differences between what she has done and what he was likely to do. In her first three years as a Justice, Sandra Day O'Connor voted with the Court's most conservative member, Justice William Rehnquist, almost nine times out of ten, or 87 per cent of the time. During the decade that Justice Stewart shared on the Court with Justice Rehnquist the two voted together in only two-thirds of the cases, or 66 per cent of the time. Given how often the Court's divisions are close ones, the potentially different vote in one-fifth of its decisions would have produced a number of important changes.

Although Justice Stewart voted with the 7–2 majority that struck down most abortion restrictions in 1973, Justice O'Connor voted with the two 1973 dissenters in one key abortion ruling a decade later, and joined three Justices in dissenting from an even closer abortion vote in another 1983 case. Her votes on abortion issues contributed to no new anti-choice majority on the Court as of 1985, but the same cannot be said of another aspect of the right to privacy: security from "unreasonable searches and seizures." In 1984, for example, in *Segura v. United States*, Justice O'Connor supported a 5–4 majority opinion that Justice Stewart almost certainly would have opposed. The case involved a nineteen-hour police seizure of Andres Segura's apartment. Acting on a tip from an arrested drug dealer, federal agents concluded early one evening that they had the legal basis, or "probable cause," to search Segura's apartment. The agents called the United States Attorney's office to obtain a search warrant, only to be told that it was too late to find a magistrate who might issue a warrant that day, and that the agents should "secure the premises" while awaiting the issuance of a warrant the next morning. The agents went to the apartment and waited as Segura entered the lobby just before midnight, handcuffed him and forced him upstairs to his apartment. When his girlfriend answered the door, the agents illegally forced their way in, searched the residence, and, finding some narcotics paraphernalia, arrested Segura, his girlfriend, and three other friends. After hauling the suspects away, the agents began a lengthy vigil in the apartment. Morning had broken, but the agents, warrantless as ever, were still rummaging through Segura's belongings. In fact, it was not until that evening, fully eighteen hours into their occupation of the residence, that the agents even went before a magistrate, who promptly issued the warrant they had failed to seek previously. When asked *why* they had waited so long, their only excuse was that they preferred to file a *typed* warrant application, and a good secretary was hard to find.

The Supreme Court's opinion acknowledged the illegality of the agents' entry but nonetheless allowed the use of the evidence, although the agents had no warrant to arrest Segura, no warrant to force their way into his apartment or to search it, and no warrant to occupy it for almost an entire day. Labeled "astonishing" by the four dissenting Justices, the result would undoubtedly have been different if Potter Stewart, rather than Sandra Day O'Connor, had cast the deciding vote. For it was Justice Stewart who, during the 1960s, had written the Court's most far-reaching opinions extending constitutional protection against just such warrantless searches. Nor is *Segura* an exceptional case: several times in 1983 and 1984, a 5–4 Court found in the Constitution's ban on unreasonable searches and seizures no obstacle to invasions that the Court, when Justice Stewart was a member, would predictably have invalidated in the name of privacy.

At the same time, Justice Stewart's more ambivalent record on questions of sex discrimination indicates that Justice O'Connor's presence might have been indispensable to the "liberal" outcome of the Court's 1981 decision in *Mississippi University for Women v. Hogan*. There, Justice O'Connor's vote was needed to create the 5–4 majority that rejected as unfairly discriminatory the exclusion of males from a Mississippi nursing school. Defying the desire of Court watchers to stuff Justices once and for all into pigeonholes of "right" or "left," this story, too, is fairly typical: when one Justice is replaced with another, the impact on the Court is likely to be progressive on some issues, conservative on others.

That complexity makes all the more crucial a sensitive inquiry into the full range of views each Justice will bring to the Court—unless, of course, one still believes that substantive views can somehow be excluded from a Justice's role. That is, as we shall see, a dangerous fantasy.

Chapter Three

THE MYTH OF THE STRICT CONSTRUCTIONIST: OUR INCOMPLETE CONSTITUTION

Some would argue that one Justice or two would not make that much difference—and that even the many 5–4 splits would gradually disappear—if the Supreme Court were staffed, as they believe it should be, with men and women who understand that constitutional adjudication is simply the job of correctly reading the Constitution. If the Justices interpret our great charter in a straightforward manner—if they pay close attention to its words and avoid twisting or stretching their meanings—there will be few occasions for controversies that can be manipulated by well-chosen appointments. All that the President and the Senate need do is stop appointing "activist" judges who impose their own philosophies upon the document they are sworn to uphold, and appoint instead properly "restrained" jurists who know, and will not exceed, a judge's proper place. So the argument goes. It is simple, appealing, and plainly wrong.

STRICT CONSTRUCTIONISM EXPLAINED

In 1717 Bishop Benjamin Hoadly told the King of England that, in his opinion, "whoever hath an absolute authority to interpret any written laws is truly the Lawgiver to all intents and purposes, and not the person who first wrote them." Thus began a controversy that has continued unabated for the last two hundred and fifty years. Not everyone has agreed that the power of judicial review gives the Supreme Court wide discretion in reading the law. Justice Joseph Story argued in 1833 that the Court must give to the constitutional text only its ordinary and natural meaning: "Constitutions are instruments of a practical nature, founded on the common business of human life, adapted to common wants, designed for common use and fitted for common understanding." A century later Justice Owen Roberts described the Supreme Court's task in an even more limited and mechanical way: "to lay the article of the Constitution which is involved beside the statute which is challenged and to decide whether the latter squares with the former."

This approach to judicial review is usually known as strict constructionism, and its guiding principle is exclusive attention to the constitutional text. The Supreme Court's Justices must take the Constitution as they find it, and not make things up as they go along. Even if the Justices are appalled by the results this method produces, or believe that the Constitution's literal commands are severely out of step with the times, it is not their job to rewrite it. That prerogative belongs to the Congress and the President—and ultimately to the people, who retain the power to *amend* the Constitution. The watchword of strict constructionism is "restraint." The continuing popularity of this approach to constitutional interpretation is revealed by the fact that President Nixon announced a policy of appointing only strict constructionists to the Supreme Court; the same "judicial philosophy" appears to be a sine qua non for nomination under President Reagan as well.

WHY IT DOESN'T WORK

The central flaw of strict constructionism is that words are inherently indeterminate—they can often be given more than one plausible meaning. If simply *reading* the Constitution the "right" way were all the Justices of the

Supreme Court had to do, the only qualification for the job would be literacy, and the only tool a dictionary. But the meanings of the Constitution's words are especially difficult to pin down. Many of its most precise commands are relatively trivial—such as the requirement that the President be thirty-five years old—while nearly all of its most important phrases are deliberate models of ambiguity. Just what does the Fourth Amendment prohibit as an "unreasonable search"? What exactly is the "speech" whose freedom the government may not "abridge"? What is it that we gain by being guaranteed the "equal protection of the laws"? And what, in heaven's name, is "due process"? Such vague phrases not only invite but *compel* the Supreme Court to put meaning *into* the Constitution, not just to take it out. Judicial construction inevitably entails a major element of judicial creation.

This is not to say that the Court is free to take the position of Humpty Dumpty, that "a word means just what I choose it to mean—neither more nor less." The Justices may not follow a policy of "anything goes" so long as it helps put an end to what they personally consider to be injustice. But the constitutional text is not enough—we need to search for, and explain our selection of, the *principles behind* the words.

Consider the First Amendment to the Constitution. Beyond dispute, it prohibits the Congress from dictating official religious beliefs, censoring newspapers, or punishing criticism of the government. The words of the First Amendment—which command that "Congress shall make no law respecting an establishment of religion, or prohibiting the free exercise thereof; or abridging the freedom of speech, or of the press"—could be read no other way. Yet not one word in the entire Constitution says that the *President* cannot do those things, even though such a notion seems unthinkable. What are we to make of this omission? A resort to the Constitution's text and *only* its text for an answer is a shortcut to a dead end. We must ask *why* the Congress is prohibited from violating our rights but the President is not. Is the President to be considered less of a threat to our liberty? Even if such a thought might have been plausible in 1791, when the First Amendment was ratified, it is certainly not plausible today: the modern American President is the repository of perhaps the world's greatest concentration of power; and that power is growing. We must look deeper than the surface of the Constitution's words.

The principle that animates the Bill of Rights, including the First Amendment, is that there are certain freedoms that are fundamental in determining the kind of society we wish to be. These freedoms must be protected from political compromise, and even democratically elected governments must fully respect them. In light of this principle, it is perfectly sensible to see the shield of the First Amendment as a bulwark of freedom against presidential as well as congressional acts. Indeed, it would be indefensible *not* to.

One of the most important problems of constitutional interpretation has been the question of the "incorporation" of the Bill of Rights into the Fourteenth Amendment, which declares that the states may not "deprive any person of life, liberty, or property, without due process of law." After the ratification of that amendment in 1868, the Supreme Court gradually recognized a glaring inconsistency in the constitutional scheme. The Bill of Rights, with its litany of fundamental liberties, had originally been understood and long been held to provide a shield only against intrusion by the *federal* government. Yet it seemed intolerable to declare that although the President and the Congress had no power to take our private property without compensation, to break into our homes and spy on us at will, or to condemn us to prison or the gallows in trials before kangaroo courts, the states remained perfectly free to do so. That position was particularly intolerable after we fought the Civil War and added the Thirteenth, Fourteenth and Fifteenth Amendments to the Constitution, in part to protect some among us from the governments of the states in which we live. Therefore, over the course of a hundred years, the Supreme Court has gradually read into the Fourteenth Amendment's

Due Process Clause most of the liberties guaranteed by the Bill of Rights. Even Justice Hugo Black, who is often considered the strictest constructionist who ever served on the Court, vigorously advocated this very practice.

Another problem emerged with the passage of the Fourteenth Amendment. That amendment, in addition to guaranteeing *due process* of law, prohibits the states from denying to anyone the *equal protection* of the laws. This latter provision was the basis of the Court's decision to strike down racially segregated public schools in *Brown v. Board of Education*. On the same day in 1954 that it upheld Brown's challenge to Topeka's segregated schools, and another student's attack on segregation in Prince Edward County, Virginia, the Court was presented with an identical challenge to the segregated schools of the District of Columbia. The problem was that the Fourteenth Amendment requires only the *states*, and not the federal government, to provide equal protection of the laws; there is no parallel provision in the Bill of Rights.

A unanimous Supreme Court recognized the absurdity of denouncing racism in Virginia while condoning it across the Potomac River in Washington, D.C., and did not hesitate to read into the Fifth Amendment's Due Process Clause—which *does* apply to the federal government—a guarantee of equal protection of the laws. The literal result of this judicial innovation was to make the Equal Protection Clause of the Fourteenth Amendment wholly redundant, for if the Fifth Amendment's Due Process Clause includes protection of equality, so must the identically worded Due Process Clause of the Fourteenth Amendment. This reading of the Constitution may seem odd indeed if one looks only at the language of the document. But the reading is perfectly logical and laudable if one examines the principles embodied in that language, for there is no defensible reason to allow the national government to run roughshod over fundamental liberties that the fifty states and their cities are required to respect.

Chief Justice Marshall once wrote that we must re-

member that "it is a *Constitution* we are expounding."
It is the grand charter of a democratic republic, the
philosophical creed of a free people, and it was written
in broad, even majestic language because it was written
to evolve. The statesmen who wrote the Constitution
meant the American experiment to endure without having to be reinvented with an endless series of explicit
amendments to its basic blueprint. There is a message
in the common adage "Ours is a Constitution of limited
powers." The Tenth Amendment makes that maxim a
reminder that the federal government in particular may
exercise only the powers ceded to it by the people in
the Constitution. Perhaps even more important, the
Ninth Amendment expressly states that even the Bill of
Rights itself is not to be understood as an exhaustive list
of individual liberties. The Ninth Amendment thereby
invites us, and our judges, to expand on the panoply of
freedoms that are uniquely our heritage. Thus the Constitution tells us, both implicitly and explicitly, that
what it does *not* say must also be interpreted, understood, and applied.

A RELATED FALLACY: THE INTENT OF THE FRAMERS

Another school of constitutional interpretation takes as
its lodestar the intent of the authors of the Constitution.
The task of the Supreme Court, when confronted by
ambiguous or open-ended language, is simply to divine
what the Framers and the authors of the amendments
had in mind. This method employs historical research
in addition to textual analysis. One obvious problem
with asking "what they meant" is that we must first
determine who "they" are. In the case of the Bill of
Rights, do we defer to the intentions of the men—yes,
it was men only—who drafted it and saw it as an essential safeguard against encroachment on fundamental freedoms, or to the intentions of those among them who
saw the Bill of Rights as unnecessary and unwise, but
acceded to its passage because otherwise some states
might never have ratified the Constitution? And how

should we understand the purpose of the Slave Trade Clause of Article I of the Constitution, which prohibits Congress from restricting the importation of slaves until 1808? Did the Framers mean by this provision that when they said, in the Declaration of Independence, "all men are created equal," they really meant "all *white* men"? Was this, too, merely a bargaining chip, a concession to the slaveholding states to entice them into the Union? Or did the Founding Fathers mean to give the South a two-decade grace period in which to phase out slavery before Congress did it for them? And how was this clause understood by the Southern legislators who ratified the Constitution?

The nagging doubt prompted by inquiries like these is that no collective body—be it the Congress or the Constitutional Convention or the aggregate of state legislatures—can really be said to have a *single*, ascertainable "purpose" or "intent." And even if such a mythical beast could be captured and examined, how relevant would it be to us today? Should the peculiar opinions held, and the particular applications envisoned, by men who have been dead for two centuries *always* trump contemporary insights into what the living Constitution means and ought to mean? Should we permit others to rule us from the grave not only through solemn enactments democratically ratified, but through hidden beliefs and premises perhaps deliberately left unstated?

Consider the Equal Protection Clause as an example. It was clearly intended to restrict racial discrimination against the recently emancipated slaves, but just what did the authors of the Fourteenth Amendment "count" as discrimination? Does a state deny equal protection by forcing blacks to attend segregated schools, use separate bathrooms, and sit only at the back of the bus? In *Plessy v. Ferguson* in 1898 a Supreme Court much closer to the source than we are today answered "no": separate but equal facilities are permissable. Half a century later a different group of Justices unanimously disagreed, because they recognized that, in a society dominated by white men, separate facilities for blacks were not likely ever to be "equal," and that, even if they were, enforced apartheid itself declared white supremacy and automatically denied equality to blacks. That decision may be hard to square with the specific, if for various reasons never expressed, agenda of those who gave us the Fourteenth Amendment. Historical evidence as to what "they" collectively had in mind is inconclusive, but it is quite possible that they had no objection to segregated schools as such. Schools even in some Northern states had been segregated for years. But public education in 1868 was not the crucial institution that it has since become. The right to own property was considered central to individual liberty, as was the right to make contracts, and we can safely say that the authors of the Equal Protection Clause "meant" to extend these rights to blacks as well as whites. In *Brown v. Board of Education* and the cases that followed it the Supreme Court was—and rightly so—less interested in the ways in which the *phrase* "equal protection" was implemented in the nineteenth century than in the sorts of inequalities which that *principle* should tolerate in the twentieth century.

ABDICATING RESPONSIBILITY FOR TOUGH CHOICES

The most serious flaw in both slavish adherence to the constitutional text and the inevitably inconclusive inquiry into the intent of those who wrote it is not just that these methods of judicial reasoning ask the wrong questions, but that they abdicate responsibility for the choices that constitutional courts *necessarily* make. The Supreme Court just cannot avoid the painful duty of exercising judgment so as to give concrete meaning to the fluid Constitution, because the constitutional rules and precepts that it is charged with administering lack that certainty which permits anything resembling automatic application. Strict constructionism in all of its variants is thus built on a conceit—which through the years has become a full-blown myth—that the Supreme Court does not *make* law, but *finds* law ready-made by others. In this mythology, the Justices do not really render their own opinions in deciding cases, for they are the mere mouthpieces of oracles beyond themselves; just as God spake by the prophets, so the Constitution speaketh by Supreme Court Justices. Even those who say they know it's not so—who claim, when wishing to sound sophisticated, that they realize some measure of choice is unavoidable—fall back on the myth when they criticize "activist" judicial decisions without specifying just *why* a particular "activist" interpretation strikes them as wrong.

Thus the members of the Court themselves occasionally duck responsibility for their substantive decisions about what the Constitution should be taken to mean by shoving the blame—or the credit—onto the document's supposedly plain words or onto the supposedly evident intentions of the people who penned those words two hundred years ago. When Chief Justice Taney declared that blacks were an "inferior class of beings" that could "justly and lawfully be reduced to slavery for the white man's benefit," he claimed that this was not *his* opinion but a conclusion dictated by the language of the Constitution and the obvious intent of the men who wrote it.

But disclaimers that "the Constitution made me do it" are rarely more persuasive than those that blame the devil. When Justice Black refused in 1967 to agree with the majority of the Court in *Katz v. United States* that the Fourth Amendment restricts the government's power to put a tap on your telephone line, it was not because *he* thought that electronic eavesdropping was acceptable, but because the plain language of the Fourth Amendment prohibits only "unreasonable *searches*," not unreasonable *wiretaps*. Naturally, such electronic invasions of privacy were not anticipated by men who knew neither telephones nor tape recorders. Such are the unwholesome fruits of what is sometimes called strict constructionism. Indeed, as the wiretap example suggests, a Constitution frozen in eighteenth-century ice would soon become obsolete; as the centuries pass, and technology changes basic patterns of life, that kind of

Constitution would melt into meaningless words signifying nothing.

Not all advocates of primary devotion to the Constitution's literal text or to its authors' historical purpose adhere resolutely to the description of those methods given here. Some searchers after the "original understanding" of the Constitution allow a radical change in circumstances over the last two hundred years to enter into the analysis; and some who seek answers to questions about the Constitution's meaning only among its clauses occasionally give weight to the way that words were used by the Framers, or to the special significance that the law has invested in certain terms. But such exceptions and variations are to no avail because, in the end, the quest for a strict constructionist remains as futile as Diogenes' search for an honest man. The judge capable of fulfilling the duty to make the Constitution meaningful to our lives, and who can accomplish this task by simply "discovering" the meanings that someone else has put there, exists only in myth. Nor does it matter whether we label the preferred method of passive discovery with such law professors' terms as "strict constructionism," "originalism," "literalism," or "mild interpretivism"; a delusion by any other name would sound as hollow. Regardless of how one labels the technique or tries to fine-tune the mechanism, there is simply no getting around the fact that whenever the Supreme Court turns to the Constitution, it must inject a lot of substantive meaning into the words and the structure, and thus the overall message, of that majestic but incomplete document. That there is much a judge could *not* properly do in the document's name is true enough. But that fact should not obscure the wide range of choices that always remain in giving the Constitution contemporary meaning.

It may be that the most subtle danger of nearsighted examination of the Constitution's text or of its authors' intentions is that, by making extremely difficult choices seem easy, such examination stops the judicial inquiry just when it becomes clear that more questions should be asked. Those crucial questions ask both *how* particular legal issues should be resolved and *who* should be trusted to resolve them. The allure of strict constructionism and of those who claim to practice it—their ability to make complicated issues sound simple and tough decisions easy—is precisely what should make us suspicious of it. For it threatens to put us to sleep at the very moments when we must be most alert to the choices that are in fact being made about the Constitution and its impact on our daily lives—choices whose shape is necessarily prefigured by the sorts of men and women we permit our Presidents to place on our nation's highest court.

Chapter Four

THE MYTH OF
THE SURPRISED PRESIDENT

The myth of the strict constructionist is an effort to
deny the powerful impact of the complex constitutional
choices the Justices cannot help making. Likewise, the
myth of the surprised President is a convenient image
that serves to deny that Presidents can have any effect
on those choices when they decide whom to nominate
to the Supreme Court. Both myths serve the same
purpose—they lull us into a state of passive acceptance
of the Presidents' nominations on the premise that the
substantive views of the nominees have no predictable
effect on their future votes as Justices or on the outcome
of the Supreme Court decisions that shape our lives.

The myth of the surprised President, however, is just
that: the historical facts will not sustain it. For while it
has been said that he who lives by the crystal ball must
learn to eat ground glass, Presidents who have tried to
leave their mark on the Court by selecting Justices with
care have only rarely found the meal unpalatable. For
the most part, and especially in areas of particular and
known concern to a President, Justices have been loyal
to the ideals and perspectives of the men who have
nominated them.

THE MYTH DESCRIBED

The myth to the contrary is, in part, a product of our
belief that Justices somehow change when they don
judicial robes. With life tenure, status above reproach

except for the drastic and remote possibility of impeachment, and the responsibility of the awesome decisions they make, Justices are seen—even by people who should know better—as shedding the biases and opinions they had before arriving at the Court. At the very least, this assumption of a judicial metamorphosis hardly applies with the same force to those Justices—60 per cent of the total so far—who served on state or lower federal courts. Yet the notion persists that appointment to the Supreme Court severs a Justice from his past. President Harry Truman adhered to this belief and declared that "packing the Supreme Court simply can't be done. . . . I've tried and it won't work. . . . Whenever you put a man on the Supreme Court he ceases to be your friend."

Truman certainly spoke from experience, for he nominated only his close friends, and two of the four men he placed on the Court voted with the majority that rebuked Truman and held that his seizure of the steel mills during the Korean War was unconstitutional. But if that is all that the myth means—that Justices are not mere minions of the Presidents who nominated them—then we can concede its undeniable truth because it is also irrefutably trivial. No one has ever argued that Justices take orders from the White House after they are appointed. But a Chief Executive who knows which issues he cares about and who is attentive can select his nominees with some confidence that he will get what he wants.

The myth of the surprised President has been sustained by some famous anecdotes of judicial independence. When Oliver Wendell Holmes, Jr., wrote an opinion that criticized the antitrust policies of Teddy Roosevelt, the man who had nominated him, a furious Roosevelt remarked, "I could carve out of a banana a judge with more backbone than that!" The consistently liberal opinions of Chief Justice Earl Warren and Justice William Brennan, Jr., so annoyed President Dwight Eisenhower that when he was asked if he had made any mistakes while President, he replied, "Yes, two, and they are both sitting on the Supreme Court." And no

President could have felt more deserted by his nominees than Richard Nixon when a unanimous Court, which included three Nixon appointees (Justice Rehnquist excused himself from the case, presumably because of his prior Justice Department role), ruled that Nixon had to comply with an order to turn over the Watergate tapes to a federal court.

The curious thing is that those who subscribe to the theory that Presidents cannot influence the Supreme Court through careful appointments always trot out the same few examples in support of their cherished myth. Yet, upon closer examination, even these famous "surprises" do not appear quite so startling. Teddy Roosevelt never forgave Holmes for his vote against the antitrust statute in *Northern Securities v. United States*, but we should remember that the law was in fact *upheld* in that case by a vote of 5 to 4: Holmes's opinion was a dissent that did not alter the outcome a bit. And on the other issues dear to President Roosevelt's heart—wage and hour legislation, child labor regulation, the labor union movement—Justice Holmes cast consistently progressive votes and gave his President every reason to be pleased.

President Eisenhower may have been displeased, in retrospect, with the performances of Chief Justice Warren and Justice Brennan. But when those appointments are judged in light of what Eisenhower hoped to accomplish in each case, the President got pretty much what he sought. Ike was not thinking about civil rights when he nominated Earl Warren; it was sufficient for him that the future Chief Justice had opposed F.D.R.'s 1937 Court-packing scheme and had endorsed the Court's rebuke to Truman in 1952 for seizing the steel mills. Besides, the appointment of Warren, the immensely popular three-term Republican Governor of California, was basically a canny political move. Warren had thrown almost the entire California delegation behind Ike at a critical moment of the 1952 Republican Nominating Convention, so nominating Warren to the Court would pay a debt. And even more important was the consideration that placing Warren on the Supreme Court would remove him from California politics, where his progressive views, independence of mind, and broad appeal to Democrats and independent voters made him a perpetual thorn in the side of the state Republican leadership, which included Richard Nixon, Ike's Vice President.

The nomination of William J. Brennan also had more to do with politics than with philosophical compatibility. When Justice Sherman Minton resigned in October of 1956, Ike saw the advantages in an election year of appointing a Roman Catholic with a working-class background from the traditionally Democratic state of New Jersey. The President was not deterred by Brennan's consistently liberal record as a New Jersey judge or by Brennan's outspoken denunciation of the reactionary Senator Joseph McCarthy. Ike was also satisfied that his nominees were highly qualified—both Warren and Brennan were appointed amid nearly universal applause. Thus neither appointment justifies the widely expressed thesis that Presidents are unlikely to get what they deliberately seek in a Supreme Court nominee.

Far from being an instance of judicial betrayal of the President who appointed them, the votes of three of Richard Nixon's Justices in the *Watergate Tapes Case* were wholly predictable. Chief Justice Warren Burger and Justices Harry Blackmun and Lewis Powell had been picked for their tough stances on "law and order"; Nixon wanted jurists who would indulge the prerogatives of prosecutors and police, rather than the rights of criminal defendants. When Nixon tried to ignore a judicial subpoena for the Watergate tape recordings, his appointees remained true to form and treated him much as they would have treated any other unindicted co-conspirator who is suspected of flouting the law—Nixon was ordered to produce the tapes. Nixon's Supreme Court appointees seem not to have made the distinction that President Reagan had in mind when, as governor of California, he remarked that those involved in the Watergate cover-up were not "real criminals." Perhaps the President who declared "I am not a crook" would have made different nominations if he had ever imagined that he himself would one day be pursued by government prosecutors.

The other often cited examples of surprised Presidents are no more convincing. Justice Joseph Story proved to be an even more committed Federalist than Chief Justice Marshall after James Madison put Story on the Supreme Court. But if President Madison, a Democratic Republican, was chagrined by Story's performance, he had only himself to blame, for most of Madison's party, including his mentor Thomas Jefferson, had warned him not to nominate Story for just this reason. There is also evidence that progressive President Woodrow Wilson knew of the latent conservative streak in his Attorney General, James McReynolds, before he nominated McReynolds to the Supreme Court. But Wilson couldn't stand having the man in his Cabinet any longer, so he "kicked him upstairs." The openly bigoted Justice McReynolds spent twenty-six years voting against everything Woodrow Wilson stood for, and compiling a record as perhaps the most reactionary and certainly the most obnoxious man who ever served on the Court. If President Wilson in fact believed that James McReynolds was a like-minded progressive liberal, then this is indeed a case of a truly surprised President, but it remains just one case out of the more than one hundred Supreme Court appointments.

Even if the other examples of surprising Justices are taken as supporting the myth, they are famous precisely because they are exceptions, and not the rule. But they do serve to illustrate an important caveat to the impact that Presidents can have on the Court. A President's ability to influence the Court's decisions hinges on how well he can foresee, prior to making the nomination, that a particular issue will arise later. On such issues of known import to a President at the time he selects his nominees, a Chief Executive is much more likely to get his way with the Court. If Harry Truman felt betrayed in the *Steel Seizure Case*, it was simply because he paid more attention to his nominees' views on the New Deal, internal Cold War security, and the civil rights movement than to their ideas about executive authority and the separation of powers. Indeed, as Richard Nixon learned, Justices may remain committed to a President's agenda even when the Executive would prefer that the Court abandon it. The historical examples that follow should remind us of the power Presidents wield when they select men and women to serve on the Supreme Court. It is a power that the nation has felt from the earliest days of the Court, right down to the decisions being rendered as these lines are written.

GEORGE WASHINGTON, JOHN ADAMS, AND THE NEW NATION

No President better understood the relationship between choosing Justices and setting the nation's course than our first Chief Executive, George Washington. Washington had one major advantage over every President who followed: he started with a clean slate, and the opportunity to fill the entire Court with men of his liking. The Constitution itself establishes the Supreme Court, but leaves the number of Justices to the Congress and the President to determine by legislation. The Judiciary Act of 1789 allowed for a Chief Justice and five Associate Justices, so George Washington had six seats to fill.

The first national government, organized after the Revolution under the Articles of Confederation, had been feeble and fractious. There is no doubt that Washington's primary goal in staffing the newly created Supreme Court was to appoint men who would be staunch supporters of the powers of the new and untried federal government. For the Court's first six Justices, Washington chose three men who had helped write the Constitution, and three who had led state ratification drives on its behalf. His choice for Chief Justice was John Jay, one of the authors of *The Federalist Papers*, a series of tracts designed to secure ratification of the Constitution in the State of New York. Washington passed over other qualified candidates who were ambivalent about the new national government, or who were advocates of strong state powers. For example, in choosing Justice James Wilson from Pennsylvania, a signer of the Constitution, the President passed over the Chief Justice of that state's Supreme Court, Thomas McKean, who was known as a leading advocate of states' rights.

From the start, Washington's Court did just what it was picked to do. After hesitating with preliminary actions in several lawsuits, the Court held, in the 1793 case of *Chisholm v. Georgia*, just what state sovereignty advocates had feared it would do and what the Constitution's proponents had promised it would not: it ruled that a citizen of one state could sue the government of another state in the Supreme Court. The states feared ruinous suits on Revolutionary War debts that they had not paid and on Tory property that they had confiscated. The *Chisholm* decision was hailed by some as an advance for the national government, and blasted by others as "annihilating the sovereignty of the states." Georgia's state assembly was so exercised by the decision that it actually made any attempt to carry out the Court's mandate a felony punishable by "hanging without benefit of clergy." And other states were so incensed by the *Chisholm* Court's rampant nationalism that Congress was persuaded to act promptly. Less than a year later Congress passed the Eleventh Amendment to the Constitution, ratified by the states in 1798, which barred future suits in federal court like the one the Supreme Court had sustained.

Washington's Justices remained committed to expanding the power of the national government. Striking down a Virginia statute concerning the repayment of British debts predating the Revolution, they ruled in *Ware v. Hylton* in 1796 that federal treaties override conflicting state laws. Later that same year, in *Hylton v. United States*, the Court upheld a federal tax on carriages over arguments that the tax did not comply with the Constitution's requirement that all direct taxes be "in proportion to the census." The broad wings of the federal taxing power remained unclipped by the Supreme Court until 1895.

The appointees of the "father of our country" faithfully fulfilled the first President's plan. Not even Washington's selection of Oliver Ellsworth as Chief Justice, when his choice of John Rutledge was rejected by the Senate, worked out badly, for Ellsworth's prompt resignation paved the way for the greatest success story in the history of Supreme Court appointments: John Adams's selection of John Marshall to become Chief Justice in January of 1801.

That selection fulfilled every federalist dream Adams *or* Washington ever had. Adams and his Federalists had just lost the Presidency to Thomas Jefferson's Democratic Republicans in the November election, and Adams was determined to leave his own man behind to run the Court. Adams's preference was to renominate John Jay, who had left the Chief Justiceship in 1795 in search of more satisfying work. Early Justices were required to ride about the country serving as circuit judges in addition to their duties in the nation's capital, and Jay loathed circuit-riding. Jay was confirmed by the Senate but declined to accept the appointment, remarking that the Court lacked "energy, weight and dignity."

Adams then turned to his crafty Secretary of State, John Marshall. The appointment was particularly irksome to President-elect Jefferson, for Marshall was his distant and unloved cousin, whom Jefferson referred to as "that gloomy malignity." Jefferson came to have more than personal reasons to dislike Marshall, for the new Chief Justice soon made the Constitution his own—with a design cut from the purest federalist cloth Adams could have asked for. As Justice Benjamin Cardozo wrote more than a century later, "Marshall gave to the Constitution of the United States the impress of his own mind; and the form of our constitutional law is what it is, because he moulded it while it was still plastic and malleable in the fire of his own intense convictions." Jefferson and his Democratic Republican successors James Madison and James Monroe occupied the White House for the next quarter of a century, but their efforts to reverse the Federalist hold on the Court were unavailing. Their six appointees to the Court were either mesmerized or overwhelmed by Chief Justice Marshall—over a thirty-year period, those six Democratic Republican Justices filed not one dissent to the key Federalist rulings of the Marshall Court. Then, in 1828, a man with a very different vision of the federal government, and the determination to see his views prevail, took charge of the White House—and the nomination power.

ANDREW JACKSON AND THE BANK

The story is one that again demonstrates a determined President's power to change history by changing the Court. The long and bitter dispute over whether the United States should have a central national bank captured the essence of the ideological struggle that split the fledgling republic: a contest between West and East, debtor and creditor, self-made man and well-born citizen, which culminated in the Presidency of Andrew Jackson. The First Bank of the United States was the brainchild of Alexander Hamilton, and the despair of Thomas Jefferson. Its twenty-year charter expired, but a Second Bank of the United States had to be created in 1816 to manage the financial aftermath of the War of 1812. The Bank was a private financial institution with national responsibilities, and it succeeded in the 1820s in establishing a sound American currency and promoting economic growth. But to frontiersman Andrew Jackson, honest citizens were farmers, mechanics, or laborers—they created the real, the tangible wealth of the nation. Bankers, by contrast, speculated with other men's earnings, and their money was not even legitimate gold and silver but highly suspect pieces of paper. If all banks were to Jackson the tools of some satanic, antidemocratic cabal known as "the money power," then the Bank of the United States was the anti-Christ, for in his eyes it corrupted legitimate enterprise throughout the nation.

The early battles over the Bank went to the Federalists—the Marshall Court upheld the Bank against attack by the states in *McCulloch v. Maryland* in 1819. In 1828 Tennessee sent its native son Andrew Jackson—the first Western President—to Washington to do battle with the Bank. The foe was not vanquished immediately. In *Craig v. Missouri* in 1830 the Supreme Court invoked the Constitution's explicit ban on state-issued currency to invalidate loan certificates issued by a state. The holding severely retarded the growth of decentralized state banks, which Jackson supported as a lesser evil than the Bank of the United States. The 4–3 majority (the Court had been expanded to seven Justices in 1807) included Chief Justice Marshall and Madison appointees Gabriel Duvall and Joseph Story. Although Jackson appointee Henry Baldwin joined the majority, Baldwin had taken his seat on the Court only a few weeks before the decision was rendered; he later recanted. Dissenting votes were cast by the senior Jackson Justice, John McLean, by Jefferson's Justice, William Johnson, and by Monroe's appointee, Smith Thompson.

Jackson vetoed an attempt to recharter the Bank in 1832, but he required a favorable judiciary to make his victory complete. Within six years of the *Craig* decision, Jackson had replaced five of the seven Justices who were on the Court when he took office. After his first attempt to place Roger Taney on the Court was defeated by the Senate the year before, Jackson succeeded in appointing Taney to replace Chief Justice Marshall in 1836. Taney was from Maryland and was an experienced veteran in the crusade against the Bank. It was Taney whom Jackson had made Secretary of the Treasury by an interim appointment while the Senate was in recess, after two previous Secretaries were dismissed for their refusal to withdraw the federal government's money from the Bank. Taney did Jackson's bidding in 1833, but was thrown out of office as soon as the Senate reconvened and refused to confirm his Cabinet appointment. Jackson acknowledged his debt to Taney and vowed revenge on his opponents.

That revenge came in 1837, when, in *Briscoe v. Bank of Kentucky*, a 6–1 Court essentially reversed the earlier holding in *Craig*. The *Briscoe* decision gave an enormous boost to state banks by upholding a state law authorizing the issuance of bank notes by a state-chartered institution. The majority included all five Jackson appointments: the three new ones—Taney, Philip Barbour, and James Wayne—and the two Jackson appointees who had served on the *Craig* Court, one of whom was Baldwin, who had returned to the fold.

Justice Story, the sole survivor of the old Marshall majority, was despondent in dissent. A friend of Story's wrote to console him, agreeing that the *Briscoe* decision was "alarming" and obviously "in collision with the case of *Craig*." President Jackson had carefully selected his nominees, even picking his hit man from the Bank fight to be Chief Justice. A rival newspaper declared "a new era is begun"—an era ushered in by Andrew Jackson's use of the nomination power. On March 3, 1837, Congress expanded the Court to nine Justices, and Jackson thus had two more appointment opportunities with which to solidify his hold on the Court. William Smith and John Catron were confirmed on the final day of Jackson's Presidency. The latter served for twenty-eight years, but the former declined his appointment because the job did not pay well enough.

It is a sobering postscript to this story that Jackson's jihad against the Bank of the United States had a very real and genuinely ironic impact on the farmers, laborers and common people for whom he took up the sword. The demise of the central banking system and consequent disruption of the nation's finances played a large part in triggering the devastating economic depression of 1837.

For the next two decades, succeeding Presidents—regardless of their political stripe—faced a cantankerous Senate that frustrated their efforts to shape the Court through appointments. Ten of the eighteen nominations made by presidents between Jackson and Lincoln failed to win Senate confirmation. During this period President John Tyler set a record for appointment failure—the Senate refused to confirm five of his six nominations. Another of our properly forgotten Chief Executives,

Millard Fillmore, came in a close second—three of his four nominations were defeated. Both Fillmore and Tyler were hampered by the fact that they ascended to the Oval Office from the Vice Presidency when their running mates—Zachary Taylor and William Henry Harrison—died not long after inauguration.

The stalemate between White House and Senate climaxed when Justice Baldwin died in April of 1844. Two Presidents sent a total of five nominations to Capitol Hill before the Senate allowed Justice Baldwin's chair to be filled—it had been empty for twenty-eight months. But if the presidential nominating power waned, it was not forgotten.

ABRAHAM LINCOLN AND THE UNION

The Supreme Court that greeted Abraham Lincoln at his inauguration in March of 1861 was considerably greyer than the one Andrew Jackson left behind, and therefore ripe for a new presidential initiative. Justice Daniel had died at age seventy-six the year before, and the preceding President, James Buchanan, had been unable to fill the seat. Justice McLean died also at seventy-six, a month after Lincoln was sworn in, and Justice John Campbell, the Court's youngest member, resigned that same month to return to his native Alabama to serve the new Confederate government. Lincoln, however, was occupied with the secession crisis and was so intent on finding Justices who would support his drive to save the Union that he waited a year before nominating replacements. In the meantime, the Court was effectively reduced to four Justices by the extended illnesses of Chief Justice Taney and Justice Catron.

When the President finally got around to nominating future Justices, he did so carefully. Lincoln eventually made five appointments; Congress gave him another seat to fill when it expanded the Court to ten Justices in March 1863, and the fifth opening appeared when Chief Justice Taney died in October 1864. Lincoln's commitment to preserving the Union required waging and winning a war of unprecedented expense and bloodshed, so he chose men likely to support both the war effort and his Union policies, even those most constitutionally suspect. For example, in 1863 Lincoln's use of his authority as Commander in Chief to order the seizure of ships before Congress had declared war was tested in the *Prize Cases*—probably the most important Civil War–era decisions rendered by the Court and, to this day, the leading decisions on the President's power to wage war. The Court sustained Lincoln's authority, but it took all three of his appointments to that date, joined by Justices Grier and Wayne, to get a majority. The four dissenting Justices, who had been appointed by three different presidents, argued that Lincoln's bold if pragmatic assertion of power was unconstitutional.

After the Civil War was over, a series of cases tested the constitutionality of Lincoln's war policies. Lincoln's appointees sometimes divided on these cases, and all five abandoned the late President's position entirely in the 1866 case of *Ex parte Milligan*, which overturned the wartime use of military courts-martial to try civilian conspirators in the North, where the regular federal courts were operating as usual. But we must remember that these cases were decided when the nation was no longer at war. Since the decisions thus in no way threatened the preservation of the Union, it was easy for the Justices to repudiate some of Lincoln's dubious assertions of executive power.

In *Ex parte Garland* and *Cummings v. Missouri* in 1867 the Court struck down, by a 5–4 margin, laws that required all citizens wishing to practice law or to run for public office or to enjoy other positions of civic responsibility to swear that they had never taken up arms against the Union or given aid to its enemies. Naturally, even fully pardoned Confederates could not swear such an oath without committing perjury, and they were therefore effectively denied full citizenship. Four of the Lincoln Justices dissented from the ruling and endorsed these laws enacted by the so-called Radical Republicans. The sole Lincoln appointee who voted to invalidate the oath requirements was Stephen Field, whose brother was counsel for one of the men who were challenging the laws. (There were only nine Justices on the bench at the time because Congress had passed a law in July of 1866 that provided for the reduction of the Court to seven members as vacancies occurred. A hostile Congress had no intention of allowing President Andrew Johnson, who succeeded to that office upon Lincoln's assassination, the chance to appoint any Justices. The Court had declined to eight members by April of 1869, when Congress created a ninth seat for President Grant to fill.)

Lincoln's Justices even endorsed his favorite legal fiction—the view that secession from the Union, the Civil War notwithstanding, had in fact never occurred. In *Texas v. White* in 1869 the Supreme Court considered a lawsuit brought by the Reconstruction government of Texas against those who had been given bonds from the state treasury in exchange for providing the Confederacy with cotton and medical supplies during the Civil War. The bondholders argued that Texas could not sue them in the Supreme Court, because only "states" could do so, and Texas, which had renounced the United States and its Constitution in 1861 and was currently occupied by the Union Army, was hardly a "state." In his opinion for the Court, Chief Justice Chase—joined by fellow Lincoln appointees David Davis and Stephen Field, as well as by Justices Nelson and Clifford—declared that Texas was most certainly one of the United States, for by law it could be nothing else. Articles of secession were null and void because the Constitution created a perpetual union and provided no means for the states to renege on their original commitment. Abraham Lincoln would have been well pleased with this holding, which echoed his first inaugural address: "the union of these states is perpetual. . . . It is safe to assert that no government proper ever had a provision in its organic law for its own termination." Four years after Abraham Lincoln was in his grave, the Justices he chose continued to give life to his vision of an indivisible Union.

It may come as no surprise that Presidents as strong and as resourceful as Washinton, Lincoln, and Jackson were able to reshape the Court to reflect their visions of the Constitution and of the nation's future. But the ability to use the nomination power to chart the course of constitutional choices is not limited to the great Presidents alone.

ULYSSES GRANT AND LEGAL TENDER

Few Presidents have entered the history books with a record as ignominious as that of Ulysses S. Grant. During his eight years in office, Grant's administration was wracked by scandal and corruption, and it is otherwise remembered only for its ineffectiveness. Yet even a President as inept and naïve as Grant can have a profound effect on the Supreme Court.

The Court's first decision on the constitutionality of the Legal Tender Acts—the laws that authorized the use of paper "greenbacks" as legal currency—is often cited by those who contend that a President has little power to affect the outcome of Supreme Court decisions. These adherents to the myth of the surprised President point out that Chief Justice Salmon Chase had been Lincoln's Treasury Secretary and, in that role, had a part in drafting the Acts during the Civil War. But, once on the Court, Chase wrote the Court's 4–3 opinion in *Hepburn v. Griswold*, which declared the Acts unconstitutional in 1870. By way of contorted and not altogether cogent reasoning, the Court held that the legislation was an improper exercise of congressional power under the Constitution's "necessary and proper" clause. President Grant and his Cabinet were outraged, for the ruling threatened their postwar economic plans to continue the use of greenbacks. Paper currency held out prospects for far greater economic growth than that possible in an economy dependent upon coins.

The myth is complete if we leave it at this point, but the story is only half told. For one thing, the three dissenting Justices were all Lincoln appointees—only two of his five appointees voted to invalidate the Legal Tender Acts. For another, the *Hepburn* decision was rendered by only seven Justices because there were two vacant seats awaiting nominations by President Grant. On the very day that *Hepburn* was handed down, Grant nominated William Strong and Joseph Bradley to fill those empty seats. In fairness to them and to President Grant, it must be noted that Grant had decided to nominate Strong and Bradley before the *Hepburn* decision was announced. But there is no doubt that Grant knew that a ruling in the case was on the way, and that the issue of paper currency was of great importance to his administration. Both of Grant's nominees were confirmed within a matter of weeks, and the Supreme Court unsurprisingly decided to hear another legal tender case. Fifteen months after *Hepburn*, the Court handed down its decision in *Knox v. Lee*, which reversed the earlier ruling. Grant's two appointees had joined the three dissenting Lincoln Justices from the *Hepburn* Court to form a new 5–4 majority that sustained the legislation and made the now familiar green currency "legal tender for all debts, public and private."

The *Legal Tender Cases* prompted the first widespread use of a phrase that had been coined to describe a proposal made a few years earlier: "packing the Court." One Washington correspondent wrote for his hometown newspaper that the lawyers who practiced at the Court had never seen anything like it. Of course, Grant denied that his judicial nominations were made to engineer this result, and we may never know the whole truth. But there can be no argument over the fact that two new Justices were on the Court, and that what had scant months before been "unconstitutional" was now "necessary and proper." It is because of a fourth-rate President's Court appointments that our pockets and purses hold wallets stuffed with paper bills rather than a few jangling coins of gold and silver.

THE ENDURING LEGACY OF HARRISON AND CLEVELAND

Two decades passed after Grant left office before any President had the chance to name more than two Justices to the Supreme Court. The next opportunity to name four men to the Court fell to another President not noted for any great contributions to our nation's history: Benjamin Harrison. If Harrison, grandson of President William Henry Harrison, is remembered at all, it is for losing the popular election in 1888 by 100,000 votes and still managing to take the Oval Office from incumbent president Grover Cleveland through the vagaries of the Electoral College. The younger Harrison was a typical Midwestern Republican politician of the times, devoted to large business interests and willing to allow the party hierarchy to run his administration for him. But his use of the nominating power was a masterful one, and an exercise whose consequences were felt into the early years of this century.

The man who preceded and followed Harrison as Chief Executive was the energetic and conscientious Grover Cleveland. Although Cleveland was the only Democrat to win the nation's highest office between the elections of James Buchanan (1856) and Woodrow Wilson (1912), he was such a dogmatic economic conservative that President Wilson regarded himself as the first real Democrat to occupy the White House since 1860. Cleveland appointed four men to the Court during his two discontinuous terms as President—Lucius Lamar, Melville Fuller, Edward White, and Rufus Peckham. With the exception of a few votes cast by Justice White, Cleveland's appointees remained true to the pro-business, pro-property, and anti-Populist views for which they were chosen.

Before the emergence of the Cleveland-Harrison Court, in decisions of the 1870s like the *Slaughterhouse Cases* and *Munn v. Illinois*, the Supreme Court had resisted the attempts of business interests to use the Fourteenth Amendment as a means of escaping state regulation. If Louisiana wanted to grant someone a state monopoly to butcher livestock, or if Illinois wished to regulate grain elevator charges to protect farmers and prevent price gouging, that was fine with the Constitution and with the Court. But by the end of the nineteenth century the Court had become a stalwart defender and promoter of the rising power of big business. In the two decades that passed between *Munn*, decided in 1877, and what was eventually recognized as the watershed case of *Allgeyer v. Louisiana* in 1897, which held that "freedom of contract" limited state power to regulate business and the economy, a major shift in the Court's membership had occurred: three of the seven Justices in the *Munn* majority (Bradley, Miller, and Swayne) had been replaced by three conservative Harrison nominees (Shiras, Brown, and Brewer); the seat of another *Munn* majority Justice (Hunt) was now filled by a Cleveland appointee (White); and Chief Justice Waite, who wrote the opinion in *Munn*, had been replaced by Cleveland's Chief Justice, Melville Fuller. Cleveland and Harrison may have been fierce political opponents from different parties, but their judicial appointments were all of a piece; these two Presidents used their nomination powers to turn the Supreme Court into the last bastion of laissez-faire capitalism.

Finally, it was Harrison Justices Brewer and Brown and Cleveland appointees Fuller and Peckham who gave decisive strength to the five-member majority that carried the day in *Lochner v. New York*. In that infamous 1905 decision, Justice Peckham declared that New York's effort to protect bakery employees by legislating a 60-hour maximum workweek violated the sacred liberty of the employer and employee to enter into whatever contracts they wished to make—a liberty protected by the Fourteenth Amendment's Due Process Clause. Out of the language of an amendment written to liberate former slaves the Justices of Cleveland and Harrison thus forged shackles to hobble government efforts to protect the health and welfare of American workers. The century had turned, Grover Cleveland had been gone from the White House for almost a decade, and Benjamin Harrison had been dead for five years. But their legacy still stalked the halls of the Supreme Court, casting a dark shadow across legislative efforts to protect laborers from economic exploitation.

WILLIAM HOWARD TAFT PROVIDES REINFORCEMENTS

Where Harrison and Cleveland left off, and after Teddy Roosevelt tried to moderate the Court's outlook, William Howard Taft resumed the task of preserving a Court set in conservative bedrock. Although he rose to the Presidency in 1908 as Teddy Roosevelt's handpicked protégé, Taft was far more conservative and much less decisive than his political mentor. Roosevelt's deep disappointment with Taft led to a bitter struggle between them for the Republican nomination in 1912: they divided their party and inadvertently gave the Presidency to Democrat Woodrow Wilson.

Taft made a record six Supreme Court appointments in his single term in office. He put five new men on the Court and elevated Justice White to the position of Chief Justice. Although he was not as dogmatic in his conservatism as the late nineteenth-century Presidents, Taft was determined to avoid nominees of the liberal stamp of Learned Hand, Louis Brandeis, or Benjamin Cardozo. Taft regarded these potential candidates as nothing less than "destroyers of the Constitution." Taft's selections buttressed the appointments of Presidents Harrison and Cleveland and ensured that the Court would remain insensitive and even hostile to the interests of working people and reformers throughout the first third of the twentieth century.

The period from 1918 to 1922 was particularly notorious in this regard, when the Court was dominated by three Taft appointees: Justices Pitney and Van Devanter, and Chief Justice White. In *Hammer v. Dagenhart*, a 1918 decision, these three remaining Taft Justices were the core of the five-man majority that struck down a federal law aimed at stopping child labor. Similarly, in *Duplex Printing Press v. Deering* in 1921 all three Justices—with Justice Pitney writing the Court's opin-

ion—helped carry a 6–3 ruling that authorized federal
courts to use the antitrust laws to suppress labor union
boycotts.

Later in 1921 Taft himself was chosen by President
Warren Harding to replace Taft's Chief Justice, Edward
White. The following year Chief Justice Taft—joined by
his two remaining appointees Pitney and Van Devanter—
authored the opinion in *Bailey v. Drexel Furniture Co.*
Bailey struck down a tax on goods made by child labor
as an illegitimate use of the congressional taxing power,
although the Court had held in 1904's *McCray v. United
States* that a congressional tax on oleomargarine was
permissible because it raised revenue. The Court was
willing to overlook what it deemed to be a "wrongful
motive" on the part of Congress when it came to regulating margarine, but not when it came to stamping out
the exploitation of children.

Although three of Taft's six appointees served for no
more than six years, the legacy of our most portly
President amounted to much more than the gargantuan
bathtub he brought to the White House. Several of
Taft's Justices were important players in this century's
early judicial contests, and the Justices whom Chief
Justice Taft pressured the weak Warren Harding to
appoint—such men as George Sutherland and Pierce
Butler—would cast decisive votes well into the 1930s.

F.D.R.: WHAT DOES COURT-PACKING REALLY MEAN?

It is one of the most popular stories in the annals of
American politics: President Franklin Roosevelt, adored
by the nation for his dynamic struggle to end the Depression, hit a roadblock in the "nine old men" of the
Supreme Court who repeatedly struck down his vital
initiatives. Plucky F.D.R. fought back, and introduced
a bill to pack the Court with like-minded Justices. But
just before the bill was to be considered, one Justice
saw the light and came over to Roosevelt's side; New
Deal lawyer Abe Fortas, later a Justice himself, dubbed
it "the switch in time that saved the nine." The

crisis passed, and both Court and country emerged unscathed.

The real story of F.D.R. and the Court requires a fuller telling—one that shows how a President can "pack" the Court in a manner at once less confrontational and more successful than the way Roosevelt originally proposed. The Court had been a major obstacle for the New Deal, unanimously striking down the National Industrial Recovery Act in 1935 in *Schechter Poultry v. United States.* In 1936 the Court dealt F.D.R. several further blows, declaring unconstitutional the Agricultural Adjustment Act and the Coal Conservation Act by 6–3 decisions in *Butler v. United States* and *Carter v. Carter Coal Co.*, and axing New York's minimum wage law 5 to 4 in *Morehead v. Tipaldo.* The *Morehead* decision came in June, when Republican Justice Owen Roberts, a Hoover appointee, was being publicly considered by the G.O.P. to run against F.D.R. in November. Roberts voted with the *Morehead* majority to strike down the minimum wage, but in July the Republican party included in its platform a provision supporting minimum wage legislation. Roberts may have felt himself to be out of step with his own party, and as it turned out, Alf Landon became the G.O.P. candidate who was to have the pleasure of being trounced by F.D.R. at the polls.

Roosevelt won by a landslide after campaigning hard against the nine old men. But with key pieces of the New Deal—the Social Security Act, the National Labor Relations Act, and unemployment compensation laws— scheduled to come before the Supreme Court in 1937, the Roosevelt administration was showing as much concern as bravado. On February 5, 1937, just a few days after an elegant White House dinner in the Court's honor, F.D.R. announced his plan to add one Justice to the Court for each Justice reaching the age of seventy, supposedly to alleviate the burden on the Court and the attitudinal problems created by the advanced age of the Justices. The Court was showing a lot of grey hair at the time, and the plan would have raised its membership to fifteen. Roosevelt would have a clear majority on the Court, and the "Four Horsemen" who had been the bane of the New Deal—Justices Van Devanter, Sutherland, Butler, and McReynolds—would be isolated in dissent. Despite this prospect, the Court-packing plan was immediately and harshly criticized from all quarters. Justice Louis Brandeis, eighty-one years old but the most dedicated New Deal supporter on the Court, was deeply offended by F.D.R.'s scheme.

But then, only a month later, Justice Roberts voted with the former dissenters to overturn the *Morehead* ruling and uphold Washington's minimum wage statute in *West Coast Hotel v. Parish*. And, the following month, by the same 5–4 margin, the Court sustained the National Labor Relations Act. In May the unemployment compensation program was also upheld 5 to 4.

Had the Court-packing plan pressured Roberts into switching? Almost certainly not, for Roberts's vote to sustain the minimum wage law was cast in the Court's December 1936 conference, *two months before* F.D.R. announced his infamous proposal. Indeed, Roberts had voted in October of that year to have the *Parrish* case argued before the Court, creating an opportunity for him to make his famous "switch in time." Most historians now attribute Roberts's switch to other factors, such as his frustrated political ambitions in 1936, when his party abandoned the more conservative tenets Roberts had tried to uphold. Beyond that, Roberts may have simply and honestly changed his mind. He was only sixty-two at the time, considerably younger than the Four Horsemen: Justice Van Devanter was seventy-eight, Justices McReynolds and Sutherland were seventy-five and Justice Butler was seventy-one. Justice Roberts was from an era different from those of his brethren, and presumably it was easier for him to change with the times.

In June of 1937 the Court-packing plan died in the Senate, and Justice Van Devanter announced his retirement. Now, the *real* Court-packing would begin. President Roosevelt, who had been denied any chance to appoint a Justice in his first term, soon enjoyed a plethora of opportunities. Within the next year F.D.R. named both New Deal Senator Hugo Black and Solicitor General Stanley Reed, the man who had defended New Deal legislation before the Court, to seats on the Supreme Court. In 1939 two members of the White House inner circle also went to the Court: Felix Frankfurter and William O. Douglas. Half of the Horsemen were gone and the transition was secure.

By 1940, when the Court considered the second Coal Conservation Act in *Sunshine Anthracite Coal Co. v. Adkins*, there were five Roosevelt Justices on the Court. The law that had been declared unconstitutional by a vote of 6 to 3 in 1936 was upheld 8 to 1 in 1940. Only Justice James McReynolds, the most stubborn and short-sighted of the Four Horsemen, dissented. That cantankerous old man left the Court in January of 1941, and a week later the Court unanimously reversed its 1918 decision in *Hammer v. Dagenhart*: Congress was now free to prohibit interstate commerce in products made with the labor of children. The next year the circle was finally closed: the new Agricultural Adjustment Act was sustained by a unanimous Court in *Wickard v. Filburn*. It was the Court's 6–3 ruling in *Butler* in 1936 that had struck down the first A.A.A., and that had begun the controversy over the Court and the New Deal.

It took F.D.R. six years to remake the Supreme Court completely. But it was the nomination power, and not the Court-packing plan, that did the job. Of course, time is not *always* a President's ally in matters relating to the Court, especially since the Twenty-second Amendment's limit of two terms as President placed a "clock" on the executive and not on the judicial branch. But when the opportunity to make appointments to the Court does arise, the prospect for constitutional changes of far-ranging impact should never be underestimated.

HARRY TRUMAN AND HIS FRIENDS

Benjamin Harrison showed us that even a mediocre President can successfully pack the Court. Harry Truman proved that even mediocre Justices can translate a

President's aims into judicial reality. F.D.R.'s Vice President likened his succession to the Oval Office upon Roosevelt's death in 1945 to the experience of being hit by a load of hay. But Truman quickly recovered and soon made the Presidency his own. Truman was a loyal politician, and in the course of forming his own administration he made many a crony appointment, including four to the Supreme Court. Two of his appointees were his former Senate buddies, Sherman Minton and Harold Burton; two were members of his executive team and close confidants: Tom Clark and Fred Vinson. Truman was lambasted in the press and on Capitol Hill for nearly all his nominations, and with good cause: with the possible exception of Justice Clark, Truman's Justices were perhaps the least distinguished group of appointments made by any President in this century.

But Harry liked his friends, and he liked their politics. He cared about three things: support for government regulatory authority, sympathy for the civil rights of blacks, and a stern appreciation of the needs of internal security during the Cold War. He got what he wanted.

Truman cared about the government's power to regulate the economy and society because his Fair Deal was essentially a gloss on F.D.R.'s New Deal. Truman's Justices had few opportunities to vindicate his—and their own—views on this score, since Roosevelt's Court-packing left the new American welfare state in a secure position. In the most famous decision on government power handed down by the Court during Truman's tenure—the 1952 *Steel Seizure Case*—two of his appointees abandoned him and made possible the Court's stern 6–3 rebuke to the President. But that unique crisis was wholly unpredictable; Truman lost because he had never thought to pick Justices who would stand with him on that as yet unforeseen issue.

But on the entirely foreseeable issues of integration and equal rights for blacks, Truman's appointees stuck by their President and gave him every reason to be pleased. In the 1948 case of *Shelley v. Kraemer*, Chief Justice Vinson wrote the opinion—joined by the other

Truman Justices—that declared that courts could not enforce racially restrictive real estate covenants designed to keep blacks and Asians out of white neighborhoods. Justices Burton, Clark, and Minton also joined Vinson's 1950 opinions requiring that blacks be admitted to a state law school (*Sweatt v. Painter*), and that they be given equal access to a public university's cafeterias and libraries (*McLaurin v. Oklahoma State Regents*). The three Truman appointees still on the Court in 1954 followed their new Chief Justice, Earl Warren, in the unanimous decision in *Brown v. Board of Education*.

As the lone Truman Justice on the Court in the 1960s, Tom Clark voted to strike down Virginia's ban on interracial marriage in *Loving v. Virginia*, and to reinstate the prosecutions of the men alleged to have murdered civil rights workers in the South in *United States v. Price*. In 1964 Justice Clark wrote the decisions in *Heart of Atlanta Motel v. United States* and *Katzenbach v. McClung*, which upheld the civil rights laws that required hotels and restaurants to accommodate blacks and whites alike.

Truman's Presidency saw the Korean War, the Berlin airlift, the birth of NATO and the advent of the Red scare. In a world peopled by conspiring Communists, Truman wanted—and got—a Court that cared mightily about internal security. As an unfortunate result, his Justices rendered some of the most repressive decisions of the twentieth century. In 1951 Chief Justice Vinson led the Court to uphold several convictions under the Smith Act, which effectively made peaceful leadership of the American Communist party a crime in itself. The same year, Justice Clark wrote the Court's opinion in *Garner v. Board of Public Works*, holding that those wishing to be administrators, janitors, or garbage collectors for Los Angeles could be denied public employment for refusing to sign an affidavit revealing whether they were members of the Communist party.

Even when only two of them were left, Truman's onetime buddies loyally maintained their hard line on the government's right to hunt Communist witches. Burton and Clark provided the decisive votes in a pair of 1958 cases that sustained the dismissals of a teacher and a subway conductor for refusing to say whether or not they were "Reds." When Justice Burton resigned later that year, Justice Clark kept the vigil alone: he wrote the opinion for the five-justice majority in yet another "Commie" disclosure case in 1959, *Uphaus v. Wyman*; and, in 1959 and 1961, Clark cast the deciding votes in cases that upheld the contempt citations of citizens who refused to "name names" and answer the wide-ranging questions of the infamous House Un-American Activities Committee. It is fortunate that many of these cases would probably be decided differently if they came before the Supreme Court today. But that probability depends to an alarming extent on the kinds of Justices who will be appointed in the future.

RICHARD NIXON'S "LAW AND ORDER"

In the two decades between Harry Truman's election and Richard Nixon's 1968 victory, the Supreme Court created controversy with rulings that expanded the rights of criminal defendants and restricted the law-enforcement methods available to police and prosecutors. Most famous was the Court's ruling in the 1966 case of *Miranda v. Arizona*, which required that suspects in police custody be apprised of their constitutional rights before interrogation. Today, it is a rare child who, having been weaned on TV crime dramas, cannot recite by heart: "You have the right to remain silent. . . ."

In response to *Miranda* and other indications that the government was supposedly going "soft on crime," Nixon's campaign for President centered on a pledge to restore "law and order" to the country. And while Nixon's Justices may have stuck to his agenda more resolutely than he wished in the *Watergate Tapes Case*, they have generally voted just as he desired to cut back the Warren Court's rulings on the rights of the accused. For example, in *Harris v. New York* in 1972, the Court, by a vote of 5 to 4, whittled down *Miranda* by allowing statements made by a suspect who has not been informed of his rights to be used in court to assail the suspect's credibility when he testifies in his own defense. The majority included the two new Nixon appointees, Warren Burger and Harry Blackmun, who had replaced two Justices (Earl Warren and Abe Fortas) from the 5–4 majority in *Miranda*. The care that President Nixon had invested in the appointment process was beginning to pay off.

The next year, Nixon appointed Lewis Powell and William Rehnquist to the Court. They formed a five-member majority—all four Nixon Justices and Kennedy appointee Byron White—to overturn a legal tradition that had endured for centuries: the twelve-person jury. In *Johnson v. Louisiana* and *Apodaca v. Oregon* in 1972 these five Justices upheld the constitutionality of criminal convictions by six-person juries and even by non-unanimous juries.

Nixon's "Get tough" policy was reliably implemented across the broad spectrum of criminal justice cases. The Court dramatically expanded the government's power to investigate citizens in 1976, when Justice Powell, joined by the other Nixon appointees, wrote the decision in *United States v. Miller* giving government agents the power to examine all of a citizen's checks and bank deposit slips without a search warrant, without "probable cause" to suspect wrongdoing, and without any warning. Three years later, in an opinion penned by Justice Blackmun, the Nixon Court gave police and prosecutors similarly unrestricted power to discover every telephone number dialed from a person's private phone. In 1984 the Nixon Justices carried out a successful raid on the long-established Fourth Amendment exclusionary rule by their decision in *United States v. Leon*, which held that evidence obtained through a legally defective search warrant may be admitted at trial so long as the police had, in good faith, a reasonable belief that the warrant was valid. It is now the law of the land that government may prosecute you with evidence that it admits it got by violating the Constitution of the United States.

President Nixon's Justices have extended his vision of

law and order past the stages of arrest and trial all the way into the prison itself. Thus Chief Justice Burger declared for a bare 5–4 majority in 1984's *Hudson v. Palmer* that inmates have no constitutional privacy rights whatsoever, and their cells, bodies, and belongings may be searched at the whim of prison officials. Such treatment is by no means limited to convicted criminals. In the same term the Chief Justice also wrote the opinion in *Block v. Rutherford*, which held that jailers could prohibit all physical contact between pre-trial detainees and their families. Without demonstrating that jail security is threatened, wardens and sheriffs can even deny a man who has been convicted of no crime the opportunity to hold his newborn daughter. The year 1984 was a particularly disappointing one for those who ran afoul of the police. Justice Rehnquist wrote for the Court in *Schall v. Martin* that juveniles who have been arrested but not yet convicted of any offense may be held without bail awaiting trial if there is a risk that they might engage in further improper activity. This indefinite pre-trial punishment is necessary in part to protect the juvenile from himself, the Nixon Court declared, even if the youngster will almost always be released immediately after a hearing, whether found innocent or guilty.

In *Rummel v. Estelle* in 1980 the Nixon Court handed down one of its most unfeeling law-and-order decisions. Billy Rummel was a Texas ne'er-do-well who committed three petty offenses. His first bust was for buying $80.00 of merchandise with a bad credit card. That earned him a sentence of three years in jail. His second offense was passing a forged check in the amount of $28.36; he got four years for that. Finally, he took $120.75 in advance payment for repairing an air conditioner, but failed to fix the thing as promised. Billy was a recidivist—a three-time loser. The People of the State of Texas had had enough, and decided to prosecute Rummel under the state habitual-offender statute. Rummel was convicted, and for his three misdeeds— his "life of crime"—he was condemned to spend the rest of his life in a Texas prison. Justice Rehnquist wrote for the five-Justice majority that a *mandatory* life sentence for three nonviolent property crimes amounting to $230 was not so "grossly disproportionate" as to amount to the "cruel and unusual punishment" prohibited by the Eighth Amendment. Having fulfilled Nixon's law-and-order hopes so well, it was Justice Rehnquist who nonetheless argued, in the speech he delivered on the eve of the 1984 election, that Presidents have enjoyed only "partial" success in packing the Court. Few could have missed the irony.

No discussion of the Nixon Court would be complete without mention of its death penalty decisions. When Justice White parted company with the Nixon camp in *Furman v. Georgia* in 1972, the Court struck down all of the death penalty statutes then in effect on the ground that they gave juries too much leeway to select individuals for execution for prejudiced reasons—or for no reason at all. The four Nixon appointees gained the upper hand in 1976, and formed the solid core of the majority that upheld rewritten death penalty laws in *Gregg v. Georgia*. But the harsh commitment to law enforcement *über alles* for which Richard Nixon picked his nominees is best revealed by 1984's *Dobbert v. Wainwright*. John Dobbert, Jr., was convicted in a Florida court for strangling his nine-year-old daughter, Kelly. The jurors voted 10 to 2 to recommend life imprisonment, but the trial judge overruled them and sentenced Dobbert to death. There was no doubt that Dobbert often beat up both Kelly and his thirteen-year-old son, John III. But as heinous as those acts were, they were insufficient under Florida law to send Dobbert to the death chamber. Dobbert could be strapped into the electric chair only for first-degree murder, and the only evidence of *that* crime was the testimony of John III, who said that he saw his father deliberately strangle Kelly to death.

Eight years after the trial, while Dobbert was awaiting execution, John recanted his trial testimony in a sworn affidavit. He said that his father did not murder Kelly, that she choked to death on her food, and that his father had even tried to give her mouth-to-mouth resuscitation. John explained that he had committed perjury because he was terrified of his father and wanted him locked up. At the time of the trial, John was also living in a children's home where he was heavily medicated with Thorazine, and he knew that the staff wanted him to testify that Dobbert had killed Kelly; John wanted desperately to please the only people who had ever been kind to him, so he lied.

The Florida courts were not persuaded by John's recantation, and Dobbert's belated trip to the electric chair was scheduled. Dobbert sought a stay of execution from the Supreme Court in order to have the Court consider an appeal. The Court declined even to take the time to give fair consideration to Dobbert's claim that he had been convicted of a capital crime on perjured testimony. In his opinion dissenting from the denial of the stay of execution, Justice Brennan wrote: "Only two men know whether Kelly Dobbert was strangled or whether she accidentally choked to death. One of them will die in several hours, the other will live with the consequences of his damning testimony for the rest of his life. Both now swear that the testimony was false. I would have thought that the federal courts would take the time . . . to minimize the risk that innocent people are put to death." Ten years after Richard Nixon had been hounded from the White House, his nominees remained on the Supreme Court, exhibiting less interest in avoiding the death of possibly innocent people than in helping government keep the grim line of the condemned moving briskly to meet their appointments with the executioner.

THE MYTH RECONSIDERED

Although history teaches that Presidents are sometimes surprised by the Supreme Court, the surprise is almost always of their own making. Presidents are surprised when Court appointment and issues are not at the top of their agendas, and when a prospective Justice's views therefore do not receive careful scrutiny from the White

House. Presidents are surprised when they are less concerned with promoting their constitutional and political philosophy than with paying political debts or accommodating geographic interests. Presidents are surprised when an issue comes before the Court that was not foreseen at the time a nomination was made, often years earlier. Presidents are surprised when a Justice, picked because of the nominee's views in an area of principal concern to the administration, holds against it on a matter to which it attached less importance. Justices are no more likely than the rest of us to have one-track minds; their opinions and attitudes run the gamut from "liberal" to "conservative" on diverse issues of political, social, economic, and foreign policy. A Justice can be a "hard-liner", on criminal justice and "soft" on abortion—or vice versa.

Nor should we forget that Justices are people, not automatic word processors. They cannot be programmed. Presidents shape the Court by guessing how particular candidates will vote in the future, and such predictions can only be based on the way the candidate has behaved and on the views he or she has expressed in the past. Previous actions and attitudes are of necessity an imperfect crystal ball, for most of us would prefer that those sitting on our nation's most august tribunal have minds capable of growth. Upon his retirement from the Court, Chief Justice Earl Warren reflected that he did not "see how a man could be on the Court and not change his views substantially over a period of years . . . for change you must if you are to do your duty on the Supreme Court." The sole dissenting vote from the notorious "separate but equal" decision in *Plessy v. Ferguson* in 1896 was cast by Southerner John Marshall Harlan. When the former slave owner was ridiculed for his evident change of mind and heart, Harlan replied that he preferred to be remembered as being right, rather than consistent.

Yet Presidents from George Washington to Richard Nixon have had success in reshaping the Court and its interpretation of the Constitution. While generalizations may fail to cover every case, some can be drawn with respect to the ingredients needed to make the Court "ripe for packing."

First, Presidents succeed in selecting nominees to their liking when they perceive that the Court as an institution is likely to be a focal point of constitutional contention, and therefore choose their nominees carefully. Both Washington, with his dream of a powerful federal government, and F.D.R., with his plan for a pervasive regulatory state, recognized that the Justices would tend the crucible wherein the future would be forged.

Second, when Presidents know that the Court will be a battleground for issues of substantive concern to them—issues such as Lincoln's war powers or Nixon's war on crime—they can typically nominate Justices whose views on these issues are known and who will hence serve as reliable champions for the Chief Executive's positions.

Third, Presidents who have particular axes to grind at the Court, as Jackson did with the Bank and as Grant did with legal tender, can make nominations that will succeed even in overturning previously explicit constitutional doctrines. It also helps a President to take office when the Justices are old, and to get as many appointments as possible in a short period of time. F.D.R. got nine in less than six years—five of them in twenty-nine months; Lincoln got five in less than three years; Grant, Harrison, and Truman each got four in four years; Nixon got four in thirty months.

Finally, it never hurts for a President's appointees to enjoy long life: five of Jackson's six Justices averaged almost twenty-seven years of service on the Court, and three of Harrison's four appointments remained on the bench for an average of fifteen years. Recognizing the importance of longevity, President Taft told his six appointees, "If any of you die, I'll disown you." Taft's influence on the Court would have been even greater had not two of his nominees, Horace Lurton and Joseph Lamar, expired after barely five years of service.

All in all, little solace can be taken from the prospect that a determined President who takes the trouble to pick his Justices with care, who selects them with an eye to their demonstrated views on subjects of concern to him, and who has several opportunities to make appointments will simply guess wrong and end up nominating a liberal in conservative garb or a conservative in liberal dress. Such rude surprises have occurred, but they are few, and a President with any skill and a little luck can usually avoid them—and can, with fair success, build the Court of his dreams.

Chapter Five

THE MYTH OF
THE SPINELESS SENATE

There is a third and final fable propagated about Supreme Court appointments. It is that even if new Justices can alter the course taken by the Court, and even if Presidents can manipulate those appointments successfully to implement their own agendas, nothing can be done about it. Appointments are the President's to make; the Senate may grumble a bit, but in the end it merely rubber-stamps the President's nominations to the Court. That is how it has always been, and that is how it must be. This is the myth of the spineless Senate. Whether the Senate *ought* to take an active role in the appointment process will be discussed in a later chapter. But as a description of historical reality, the myth of the spineless Senate holds no larger a measure of truth than do the other two myths we have explored. The plain fact is that the Senate has vigorously exercised its power to provide "advice and consent" on Presidents' Court nominations since the time the very first Justices were selected.

THE MYTH DEFINED

On Election Night, 1984, when President Ronald Reagan proclaimed, "Tonight is the end of nothing; it's the beginning of everything," he was right, at least with respect to the potential selection of new Justices for the Supreme Court. But, begin as the new President might, the Senate has frequently been unwilling to exchange a President's electoral mandate for a blank check to assemble the Court of his dreams.

Justices help govern the nation, and lay down the ground rules for the rest of government, long after the Presidents who appointed them have left the White House. Seats on the Court thus cannot be viewed as merely slots in a second Cabinet. Notwithstanding a 1984 Republican campaign brochure that listed Justice Sandra Day O'Connor as "one of the eight outstanding . . . women executives of the Reagan Administration," the Justices are *not* appointed to serve the President; as fervently as some Presidents have wished that the Court were but another executive agency, the Justices remain the leaders of an equal and independent third branch of government, one designed more to *check* the executive branch than to do its bidding. It should therefore come as no surprise that the Senate has rejected a higher proportion of presidential nominations for Supreme Court Justice than for any other national office. Almost *one out of every five nominees* to the Court has failed to gain the Senate's "consent." No other nomination that a President makes receives more rigorous scrutiny.

And yet there is a myth of the spineless Senate—a fable that the Senate has historically treated Supreme Court nominations much like a President's choice of Attorney General or even of Postmaster General, usually deferring and giving the Chief Executive the "man he wants." That myth could persist in the face of one historic counter-example after another only because many have been swayed by a basic misperception of the constitutional structure of the appointment process: many have evidently forgotten that a President's naming of a candidate is only half the procedure; the President's choice must also receive the "advice and consent" of the Senate. Only executive nomination *plus* senatorial confirmation equals appointment. The myth that Senate confirmation is a mere formality has been nurtured by intermittent periods of relative peace between Senate and White House, when candidates have either been opposed unsuccessfully or not opposed at all. And, in recent times, the myth has drawn unwarranted credi-

bility from the fact that the five Justices from Justice
Blackmun in 1970 through Justice O'Connor in 1981
were in fact confirmed by a vote tally of 448 to 27, with
all but Justice Rehnquist having received almost unanimous approval.

Like other myths, that of the spineless Senate has
sometimes served to reinforce itself by undermining
the Senate's attempts to take an active role in the
appointment process. At times, the myth has in this
way become a self-fulfilling prophecy. And even when
it has not, it has occasionally clouded a clear view of the
Senate's traditional role. Thus, during the most recently contested nomination, that of Judge G. Harrold
Carswell in 1970, one member of the Senate Judiciary
Committee counseled that the Senate simply had no
right to "withhold its advice and consent in the absence
of clear evidence that the nominee is not qualified."
But in the end the Senate acted on a broader conception of its place in the system of checks and balances.
And the fact is that the Senate has been doing just that
for one hundred and seventy five years.

THE CONSENT OF THE SENATE

As we near the celebration of our Constitution's bicentennial in 1987, we also approach a less exalted anniver-
sary: the two hundredth year since the Senate first
refused to give its consent to a Supreme Court nomination. When Chief Justice John Jay left the Court in
1795, Justice John Rutledge had already resigned to
become Chief Justice of South Carolina—a reminder of
how far the nation's Supreme Court had to go before
reaching its later prominence. As a distinguished jurist
and one of the principal authors of the first draft of the
Constitution, Rutledge was plainly qualified for the post
of Chief Justice of the United States. George Washington nominated Rutledge and was so confident of a speedy
confirmation that he had the formal commission papers
drawn up.

But it was not to be. A few weeks after his nomination, Rutledge attacked the Jay Treaty—a conciliatory treaty negotiated by the Washington administration to ease tensions with Great Britain. The treaty was ardently supported by the Federalists, Washington's Senate allies, as an integral part of party policy; it was opposed by Democratic Republicans as an affront to the nation's former ally, France. To the minds of many Senators, Rutledge's opposition to the treaty called into question his views on foreign policy and his judgment in taking so strident a position on an issue that polarized the nation. Rutledge's behavior even fueled rumors that he suffered from mental instability.

The opposition to Rutledge's nomination was led by a fellow Federalist, Oliver Ellsworth. Ellsworth has been called the Father of the Federal Judiciary because he sponsored the Judiciary Act of 1789, which established a system of lower federal courts and set the size of the Supreme Court. Although he hardly anticipated it at the time, Ellsworth later became Chief Justice in Rutledge's stead, keeping the nation's highest judicial seat warm just long enough for President Adams to name John Marshall to the post that Rutledge might otherwise have held into the 1800s. Ellsworth's opposition to Rutledge firmly established that, right from the start, those who wrote the Constitution and founded our nation had no doubt that inquiry into a candidate's substantive views was a proper and even essential part of the confirmation process.

The debate over Rutledge raged in the country, the press, and the Senate for five months while he continued to preside over the Court by virtue of the interim appointment Washington had made while the Senate was not in session. Rutledge was ultimately rejected by a vote of 14 to 10, as much by his own party as by the Senators of the opposition. Even the insistence of the Father of our Country himself was insufficient to overcome the Senate's decision to exercise independently its power of confirmation.

THE ADVICE OF THE SENATE

The Senate's role in the appointment process entails more than the exercise of the veto power over nominations. In addition to giving the Senate the power to withhold its consent to Supreme Court nominations, the Constitution directs that the President's appointments be made with the "advice" of the Senate. Sometimes this has meant that the President has actually turned to the upper house of Congress for suggestions as to whom to nominate. On other occasions a President unable to win confirmation of his candidates has lobbied key Senators for assistance and submitted names to them for approval. Grover Cleveland did this with regard to Justice Rufus Peckham in 1895, after powerful New York Senator David B. Hill led the Senate to ax two previous Cleveland nominations.

Nor have Senators always waited for the President to come to them for advice. In 1869 a large majority of both the Senate and the House of Representatives signed a petition that persuaded President Grant to nominate Edwin M. Stanton. But the Senate's most aggressive exercise of its power to advise the President on appointments came in 1932, when Justice Holmes announced his retirement. The chairman of the Judiciary Committee, Senator George Norris, immediately made it clear to President Hoover that he and his fellow committee members, mostly Democrats and Progressive Republicans, would insist upon a liberal jurist in the Holmes mold.

Others were more specific: law school deans, labor leaders, and businessmen all urged Hoover to nominate Chief Judge Benjamin Cardozo of the New York Court of Appeals. Cardozo was not only a distinguished jurist but also perhaps the most insightful—and certainly the most erudite—legal scholar of the day. When Hoover demurred, the Chairman of the Foreign Relations Committee, Senator William Borah—whose support Hoover needed in other matters—paid a visit to the White House. On the eve of the day Hoover had scheduled for the announcement of his nominee, he met with

Borah and handed the proud and powerful Senator a list on which were ranked the President's candidates in descending order of preference. Cardozo's name was at the bottom. Borah glanced at the list and remarked, "Your list is all right, but you handed it to me upside down." The President argued that the Court already had two New Yorkers and one Jew: the addition of the Jewish Cardozo was bound to cause more trouble with the anti-Semitic Justice McReynolds, who expressed his bias to the President in no uncertain terms. Senator Borah dismissed the geographic considerations and sternly informed Hoover that anyone who would raise the issue of Cardozo's religion was "unfit to advise you in so important a matter." Hoover caved in and Cardozo's nomination was confirmed by acclamation a few days later.

Thus, far from always rubber-stamping presidential nominees, the Senate sometimes has even gone beyond rejecting candidates from its perch on Capitol Hill, and has actually stormed the Oval Office to bestow upon the President the boon of senatorial "advice."

CRONIES AND MEDIOCRITIES

No one doubts the propriety of a Senate refusal to confirm a nominee who is patently unqualified to serve as a Justice. The Senate has frequently hesitated to confirm and occasionally has even rejected candidates who reveal a lack of legal accomplishment and learning or a dearth of proper judicial temperament. Alexander Wolcott, a Connecticut boss of the Democratic Republican party, was the first nominee to be rejected primarily because he was not up to snuff. When Wolcott's name was submitted by James Madison in 1811, one Washington correspondent for a leading newspaper dubbed the nomination "abominable," and even a Senate completely controlled by Madison and Wolcott's own party (28 of 34 Senate seats) could not bring itself to accept the "President's man." Wolcott was rejected 24 to 9.

Rejection of mediocre candidates for the Court is not an exclusively ninteenth-century phenomenon. After his nomination of Southerner Clement Haynsworth was rejected by the Senate in November of 1969, President Nixon's revenge was the nomination of G. Harrold Carswell. During the course of Haynsworth's confirmation hearings, several Senators had raised ethical questions about a case in which the nominee had participated as a federal appellate judge even though he had a financial stake in one of the companies involved. Haynsworth was also opposed by labor, minorities, and civil rights groups. Nixon apparently decided to use his next nomination to teach the Senate a lesson at the expense of the Supreme Court; unlike Haynsworth, who was a judge of some distinction and whose integrity may in fact have been unfairly denigrated, Carswell, also a Southern federal judge, was a lawyer most memorable for being eminently forgettable. During his tenure as a federal judge, Carswell compiled an almost unequaled record for being reversed by higher courts, and earned a solid reputation for shallow and dubious rulings. Even Carswell's supporters in the Senate had difficulty finding good things to say about the nomination. Senator Roman Hruska defended Judge Carswell on the floor of the Senate by saying, "Even if he is mediocre, there are a lot of mediocre judges and people and lawyers. They are entitled to a little representation, aren't they?" With such friends, Carswell needed few enemies. A bipartisan coalition of Senators answered the Hruska query when they defeated the nomination by a vote of 51 to 45.

The Senate has ways of blocking Supreme Court nominations other than by straightforward rejection in a confirmation vote. President Grant's nomination of his Attorney General, George Williams, provides an example. When Grant sent Williams's name to the Senate in late 1873, about the most one could say of Williams was that he was honest and dedicated—outstanding characteristics in the corrupt Grant administration, to be sure, but hardly sufficient credentials for service on the highest court in the land. The Senate killed the Williams nomination by simply refusing to act upon it until the embarrassed nominee asked President Grant to withdraw his name from consideration.

When nominees of marginal talents survive senatorial challenge and take their seats on the Court, sometimes even the Presidents who put them there eventually have cause for regret. President Taft was less concerned with Mahlon Pitney's dubious intellectual gifts than with the nominee's rigidly conservative political philosophy—a philosophy to which Pitney later adhered as a Justice. Since Pitney, like Taft, had no fondness for labor unions and despised government regulation, his name was dispatched to Capitol Hill in 1912. A handful of Senators more concerned about legal acumen managed to hold up confirmation for a month, but in the end Justice Pitney took a seat on the Court.

Pitney was still there a decade later when Taft himself was appointed Chief Justice. Now that he had to work with the man and saw the effects of Pitney's jurisprudence firsthand, Taft began to see the wisdom of those Senators who had fought the nomination. Although Justice Pitney continued to cast votes the way Chief Justice Taft liked, Taft publicly pronounced Pitney to be a "weak member" of the Court to whom he could "not assign cases."

Mediocrity sometimes finds its way onto the Supreme Court when Presidents are more concerned with rewarding loyal friends than with augmenting the Court's legal talent or affecting its ideological tilt. President Chester Arthur pioneered the merit system in national government appointments and authored the Civil Service Reform Act of 1883. But he had a relapse in 1882 and nominated his mentor and former boss, arch political spoilsman Roscoe Conkling, to the Court. While Senator Conkling mulled over the prospect, both nominee and nominator received a thorough roasting in the press. Amid widespread recognition that Conkling was unfit for the office, the Senate adhered to its tradition of always affirming its own and confirmed the nomination 39 to 12. President Arthur and the nation were spared a potentially disastrous appointment when Conkling capitulated to collective wisdom—and his better judgment—and declined the honor five days after his confirmation.

Not all tales of Senate efforts to prevent Presidents from filling the Court with their undistinguished chums have such happy endings. Remember, President Truman appointed four men to the Court, and all were his loyal friends and advisers. The Senate allowed Truman's first two nominees—former fellow Senator Harold Burton, and confidant and Treasury Secretary Fred Vinson—onto the Court without major objection. But the Senate balked at Truman's cronyism when he nominated his Attorney General and trusted domestic adviser, Tom Clark. One periodical characterized Clark as a "second-rate political hack who has known what backs to slap and when," and sarcastically concluded that it was appropriate that "the least able of Attorneys General of the United States should, as a result of raw political favoritism, become the least able of the members of the Supreme Court." In a 78-3 vote that does not reveal the depth of the controversy, the Senate nevertheless confirmed Clark.

Justice Clark's initial performance on the bench fulfilled the predictions of his detractors: he was ill at ease, unimaginative, and inclined to conformity. It is to Justice Clark's credit that he matured somewhat in his years on the Court; he even outgrew his authoritarian tendencies enough to cast the decisive vote, and to write the opinion in favor of the exclusionary rule, in *Mapp v. Ohio*. But it would be a serious mistake to expect that every weed will someday blossom and bear rich fruit. More typical by far is the experience of Truman's final appointee, his devoted personal and political friend, former Senator Sherman Minton. Despite the Senate's historic practice of nearly automatic confirmation of its own members and alumni, several Senators called on Minton to appear before the Judiciary Committee. Minton declined the "invitation" and said that he would stand on his record as a Senator and a federal appellate judge. In the end the Senate was unable to bring itself to reject its jovial alumnus; Minton was confirmed 48 to 16.

Justice Minton's seven years on the Court were not memorable. He earned the affection of his colleagues and did his share of work, but wrote no opinions of lasting importance and usually just went along with other Justices. Minton's record, as well as that of Truman's other appointments, demonstrates the wisdom of the proposition that Justices ought to be much more than just nice guys and loyal friends.

None of this is to say that anyone who knows the President personally or holds office in his administration is therefore a "crony" undeserving of appointment to the Supreme Court. The difference between a crony and an accomplished candidate who happens to be a friend or an adviser of the President is like the difference between a celebrity who is famous for being famous, and a celebrated actress who is famous for her talents. Felix Frankfurter was a member of F.D.R.'s inner circle when Roosevelt nominated him to the Supreme Court. But the future Justice Frankfurter had come to the President's attention through his major scholarly writings on government regulation and through the pathbreaking course that Frankfurter had initiated at the Harvard Law School—a course which taught the first comprehensive and integrated approach to government regulation and administration. The Frankfurter nomination was unanimously confirmed.

The rise of one of L.B.J.'s nominees, Homer Thornberry, was quite different. Thornberry was an old pal, who had been mayor of Austin, Texas, and had held President Johnson's former seat in the House of Representatives for several terms. Thornberry was a decent public servant of modest abilities who knew the right people at the right time. L.B.J. first made Thornberry a federal district judge and then appointed him to the court of appeals. When the President proposed a further promotion to the Supreme Court in the summer of 1968, even Democratic Senators decided that enough was enough. The nomination met a quiet death in the Senate when Justice Fortas, whom Thornberry was to have replaced, was not elevated to Chief Justice. If any further evidence of Thornberry's unsuitability for the

Supreme Court is needed, it should be noted that he later supported Nixon's nomination of Harrold Carswell.

Presidents who have nominated people to the Court for no better reason than that the nominee is the President's pal have often encountered Senates that felt they could reject such nominees for that very same reason. Presidents who wish to reward their friends and supporters should appoint them to be deputy assistant under-secretary of something, or even to be head of a Cabinet-level department, *not* to be a life-tenured Justice of the Supreme Court.

Opposition to and rejection of nominees on the basis of qualification has not occurred more often for three reasons—two good and one bad. First, most Presidents have figured out that the Senate is not bound to confirm manifestly inferior choices. Second, Presidents who want to leave a constitutional legacy by shaping the Court usually have more sense than to invest that hope in a jurist who is not equal to the task. Finally, and sadly, the Senate has at times been unwilling or unable to muster sufficient concern to force a President to raise his standards—and his sights—when selecting nominees. Given what is at stake every time a Justice is appointed, such deference—whether born of respect for the Chief Executive or of simple sloth or lack of spine—is surely out of place. The questions that confront the Court today and will continue to confront it into the twenty-first century place extreme demands on the energy, the wisdom, and the analytic talents of the Justices. Not one of this century's most esteemed Justices—Holmes, Cardozo, Brandeis, Hughes, Stone, Frankfurter—was merely a crony or solely a political appointee. Some were esteemed as first-rate academics, some were accomplished and eclectic jurists, some were distinguished lawyers and public servants—and all have earned respect across the entire breadth of the political and ideological spectrum. All of them were learned in the lessons of the Constitution's past, and each of them had his own broad vision of the Constitution's future.

ON PHILOSOPHICAL GROUNDS

The Senate's rejection of the nomination of John Rutledge in 1795 began a tradition of inquiry into the political views and public positions of candidates for the Court. Democratic Republican Senators objected to John Quincy Adams's nomination of Robert Trimble in 1826 on the ground that, despite his affiliation with their own party, Trimble hewed too consistently to the Whig party line by favoring federal over state power. Trimble was confirmed only after an acrimonious battle in the Senate.

Justice Trimble died after but two years of service, and Adams's attempt to replace him with former Senator John Crittenden, a Whig follower of Henry Clay, met stiff resistance in December of 1828. Jacksonian democracy had been swept into national government by the election of the month before, and Crittenden's moderate Whig notions of federal supremacy were unacceptable to the Senate. Crittenden's nomination, despite his alumnus status, was postponed—and thereby consigned to oblivion—in February of 1829, a few weeks before Andrew Jackson's inauguration.

Jackson himself encountered Senate opposition to some of his nominees. Vice President John Calhoun and his Senate allies could not abide the high-tariff policy advocated by Congressman Henry Baldwin. Calhoun succeeded in blocking Jackson's attempt to appoint Baldwin Secretary of the Treasury, but could only delay Baldwin's Court nomination for a few days. In January of 1830 the Senate took up the matter and confirmed Baldwin's appointment to the Court.

The Senate's Whigs defeated Jackson's first attempt to put his trusted henchman Roger Taney on the Court in January of 1835 by postponing consideration of the nomination on the last day of the Senate's session in March. A further effort to keep the hated nemesis of the Bank of the United States off the Court, by legislating the vacant seat out of existence, passed the Senate but died in the House. Jackson bided his time and submitted Taney's name again in December of 1835, this time to replace Chief Justice Marshall.

The Whigs still vigorously opposed Taney's views on the Bank, and they found allies in the followers of Vice President Calhoun. Senator Henry Clay, the "great compromiser," was said to use every "opprobrious epithet" in his vocabulary to fight the Taney nomination. Although the Senate's lions—Webster, Clay, Calhoun—roared to the very end, they were unable to marshal sufficient support, and Taney became Chief Justice by a vote of 29 to 15.

The fact that the Senate's leaders lost their struggle to keep Taney off the Court should not obscure the equally significant fact that they had no reservation about opposing a candidate on the ground that they believed his views did not belong on the Court. As Senator Borah, who led the fight against John Parker's nomination in 1930, put it:

> They opposed [Taney] for the same reason some of us now oppose the present nominee, because they believed his views on certain important matters were unsound. They certainly did not oppose him because of his lack of learning, or because of his incapability as a lawyer, for in no sense was he lacking in fitness except, in their opinion, that he did not give proper construction to certain problems which were then obtaining.

President James K. Polk nominated Pennsylvania Judge George Woodward in December of 1845. Woodward was considered an able jurist, and with the Senate in the hands of his party (31 Democrats to 25 Whigs), Polk expected quick and easy confirmation. But Woodward was a maverick Democrat who supported the American Nativist agenda, which called for restricted immigration and discrimination against new ethnic groups. The Democratic party had repudiated the Nativist agenda in its 1840 and 1844 platforms; that agenda was nowhere a greater anathema than in states such as Woodward's own Pennsylvania, which already had large ethnic populations.

Woodward's views came into the glare of public scrutiny when a newspaper published an account of some remarks he had made, which included "certain Native American expressions about Irish-Americans." One member of the local bar wrote to a Justice that Woodward was not "sound on all constitutional questions." The Senate stewed over the nomination for a month, while Polk urged Democratic Senators to stick with his choice.

In the end, only 19 of the Senate's 31 Democrats supported the Woodward nomination—it was defeated 29 to 20. A decade before the decision in *Dred Scott v. Sandford*, the Senate had begun to draw the line on intolerance.

A similar but even more passionate objection was raised against President Buchanan's nomination of Nathan Clifford in the wake of *Dred Scott* in 1857. Clifford, Polk's Attorney General, not only apologized for slavery but defended it. The Senate's abolitionists and their allies went gunning for Clifford and waged a fierce five-week battle against his nomination. Only the Democrats' last-minute success in closing ranks, and the fortuitous absence of Republican Senators Charles Sumner and Simon Cameron, brought about Clifford's confirmation by a narrow margin, 26 to 23.

The abolitionists were more successful with Buchanan's second and last nominee, Secretary of State Jeremiah Black. Black had been Chief Justice of the Pennsylvania Supreme Court and Attorney General of the United States, and Buchanan wanted an appointee with an impressive résumé and moderate views. Part of Buchanan's problem was that he was a lame duck President when he nominated Black in February of 1861. The outgoing President was making one last stab at accommodating the rift between North and South, even though the Southern states had already begun to secede. Many Senators, on the other hand, were determined to keep the vacancy open—to be filled by President-elect Lincoln. But Black's real liability in the confirmation contest was that he opposed the outright abolition of slavery—not a popular position on the eve of the Civil War. The fact that Lincoln's own position on slavery at that time was not too different from Black's did not deter the Senate from rejecting Black, but by only one vote: 26 to 25.

A nominee's views on slavery remained a hot topic for Senate inquiry even after the surrender at Appomattox. Grant's choice of Caleb Cushing to succeed Salmon Chase as Chief Justice foundered on those same shoals in 1874. Possessed of a fine mind and undoubtedly highly qualified for the position, Cushing was perceived by the Senate as too quick to change his political stripes to suit the times. When captured Confederate documents revealed that Cushing—perhaps hedging his bets, perhaps merely fence-sitting as usual—had corresponded with Confederate President Jefferson Davis, and had even recommended a friend for a post in Davis's rebel government, the Radical Republicans in the Senate had a field day. President Grant withdrew the Cushing nomination before the Senate could reject it. The discovery of those Confederate documents in 1874, like the 1846 report of George Woodward's ethnic slurs, proves that the Senate has a long history of doing its homework on potential Supreme Court Justices.

Contemporary Senates still inquire into a nominee's position on civil rights for blacks. As we saw, Judge Haynsworth's alleged insensitivity to civil rights litigants contributed to his rejection in 1969, although it was probably the then recent Fortas affair that doomed Haynsworth, and would probably have doomed any other nominee about whom so much as an ethical eyebrow could be raised. Whatever may be the case as to Clement Haynsworth, the picture is quite clear as to Harrold Carswell, whose 1948 campaign pledges to support white supremacy surfaced during his confirmation hearings in 1970. Further evidence clinched Carswell's reputation as a racist: during his tenure as a United States Attorney, Carswell had facilitated the conversion of a public golf course into a private club so that it could continue to exclude blacks.

Sensitivity about a nominee's views on racial integration has cut both ways during confirmation struggles. President Eisenhower's appointment of Justice Potter Stewart was delayed for four months in 1959 by a group of Southern Senators who were alienated by Stewart's candid comments to the Judiciary Committee that he had no intention of voting to overturn *Brown v. Board of Education.*

The Senate has also fought over a candidate's attitudes toward business and the economy. Senator Stanley Matthews, a corporate attorney who continued to represent railroads even after his election to the Senate, was criticized in January of 1881 for being excessively sympathetic to business interests, and the Senate simply refused to act on the nomination by the outgoing President Rutherford B. Hayes, even though the nominee was one of its own members. When President Garfield renominated Matthews later that year, he was confirmed—but by the slimmest of margins: 24 to 23. On the other side of the coin, to mint a phrase, Grant nominee Joseph Bradley's dedication to "soft money" or greenbacks came under fire from Eastern "hard currency" business interests before Bradley was confirmed in 1870.

One need not endorse the opinions espoused by those Senators who cast negative votes on confirmation, nor disagree with the positions taken by the nominees who suffered those rejections, in order to accept the irrefutable historical evidence that, for reasons both good and bad, the Senate has long judged candidates for the Supreme Court on the basis of what they believe.

SEEKING A BALANCE ON THE COURT

There have been times when the Senate's concern over a candidate's position on important issues has focused as much on the net impact of adding the candidate to the Court as on the opinions of the nominee himself. In March of 1930, Herbert Hoover nominated federal Judge John Parker of North Carolina. Progressive Northern Republicans, disturbed by the direction taken by the

Court under Chief Justice Taft, began to organize opposition to Parker.

Parker's opinion for the Fourth Circuit Court of Appeals in the *Red Jacket Mining Company* case drew attention to his stand on labor activism. In that ruling, Parker upheld a "yellow dog" contract that set as a condition of employment a worker's pledge never to join a union. The workers' petition to the Supreme Court was unanimously rejected, and Parker's opinion was generally recognized to be in line with the High Court's holdings on the question.

One magazine characterized the issue in Parker's nomination as a concern that "dogmatic adherence to a judicial precedent . . . is not evidence that a man is fit to sit on the Supreme Bench." Opponents argued that Parker should have been strong enough to see that yellow dog contracts were unjust and to rule just that, despite precedents to the contrary. The pro-labor campaign to reject Parker was thus based not on any claims of incompetence by Parker, but on an abhorrence of the anti-labor judicial doctrine of the 1920s, and an objection to the highly conservative, anti-labor majority that already existed on the Supreme Court.

Civil rights activists—among the first in what later became a grass-roots movement—also organized to oppose Parker. They brought out racist statements made by the nominee when he ran for governor of North Carolina. Among them were Parker's suggestion that "the negro . . . does not desire to enter politics" and his characterization of black participation in government as "evil." Oswald Villard, a staunch supporter of black causes, declared that the Senate would no longer play a purely negative role in the appointment process, but would henceforth seek to direct the Court in a more progressive direction to counteract conservative presidential nominations. Parker was denied a seat on the Court by a vote of 41 to 39.

Justice William O. Douglas later wrote that, in his opinion, John Parker was a more capable man and would have made a better Justice than the man appointed in his place, Owen Roberts. But the Senate that rejected Parker was less concerned with his qualifications, or even his opinions when considered in isolation, than with what the addition of a man like Parker would do to a Court that already inclined toward the reactionary. Justice Roberts, of course, was less wedded to the wisdom of the past; his was the famous "switch in time" vote of 1937 that, as we saw, helped defuse the Court-packing crisis. In 1930 the Senate deployed its power of advice and consent to keep the Court from sliding further along what it perceived to be an inappropriate constitutional course.

TAKING STOCK OF THE MYTH

In 1970 liberal Republican Senator Charles Mathias of Maryland objected that persistent inquiries into Judge Carswell's views on racial equality were improper and showed a lack of respect for "the principle of judicial independence." Following Carswell's rejection, President Nixon publicly complained that he had been unfairly denied what the Constitution gave him and what every other President had been accorded—the "right" to see his nominees appointed. The record of the appointment process since the dawn of the republic clearly reveals that both men were wrong.

Far from being uniformly spineless, the Senate has frequently been willing to exercise its constitutional authority to scrutinize the judicial and philosophical inclinations of the President's nominees. There is no doubt that the Senate has sometimes abused its power. The unsuccessful opposition to Woodrow Wilson's nomination of Louis Brandeis in 1916 was fueled as much by anti-Semitism as by legitimate objections to the nominee's progressive philosophy. Equally improper, but quite amusing, was the case of North Dakota Senator William Langer, a senior member of the Judiciary Committee in the 1950s. For six years, Langer conducted a lonely and quixotic campaign of opposition to any and all nominees to the Court in order to protest the fact that no one from the great State of North Dakota had ever received an appointment. Presidents Tyler and Fillmore compiled their deplorable records of Senate rejections less because the caliber of their Supreme Court nominees was questionable than because the Senate took advantage of the political weakness of Tyler and Fillmore as unelected Presidents. President Andrew Johnson faced the most uncooperative Senate in American history—the Radical Republicans in all probability would not have confirmed Solomon himself had Johnson named him to serve on the Court.

But occasional abuses or periods of acquiescence do not refute the simple truth that the upper house of Congress has been scrutinizing Supreme Court nominees and rejecting them on the basis of their political, judicial, and economic philosophies ever since George Washington was President.

Chapter Six

POLICING THE OUTER LIMITS: TESTING NOMINEES ONE BY ONE

Whether a nominee is fit to serve as a Supreme Court Justice is a question that can be responsibly answered only after a thorough examination of the nominee's basic outlook and ideas about the law, as well as a critical assessment of the nominee's character and intellect. In September of 1981, the Senate Judiciary Committee held hearings on the confirmation of Arizona Judge Sandra Day O'Connor, who had been nominated by President Reagan. Senator Joseph Biden outlined the three questions the committee hoped to answer: Does the nominee have the intellectual capacity, competence, and temperament to be a Supreme Court Justice? Is the nominee of good moral character and free of conflicts of interest? Will the nominee faithfully uphold the Constitution of the United States?

Each of the questions is appropriate, but even collectively, they do not go far enough. As we have seen, the Constitution gives the appointment power to the President and the Senate *together*: one nominates and the other confirms. The Senate's constitutional obligation to provide "advice and consent" in the appointment of the High Court's members can be fulfilled only by a more searching inquiry. Each Senator, as well as the President, should determine the outer boundaries of what is acceptable in terms of a potential Justice's constitutional and judicial philosophies—a candidate's substantive views of what the law should be, and the candidate's institutional views of what role the Supreme Court should play. We have come to accept as fact that the President is free to nominate only those candidates who come within his broad circle of specifications. We should accept equally the fact that the Senate collectively, and each Senator individually, is free to confirm only those who fall within the ambit of criteria fashioned by the Senate, and indeed by each Senator. In the end, Justices would be appointed—as they *should* be—only from the area where these circles overlap.

THE NOMINEE'S VISION OF WHAT THE CONSTITUTION MEANS

A cartoon appeared not long ago about a bored Supreme Court that decided, as a lark, to hold that the Constitution actually delegated the legislative power not to Congress but to the staff of the National Zoo. Although no one who seriously entertained so absurd an idea would ever be nominated, the range of opinion among judges, scholars, and lawyers on supposedly settled issues of constitutional law is so broad that outer limits need to be set considerably short of the absurd. For example, the Senate's hearings on the nomination of Assistant Attorney General William Rehnquist revealed that, as a law clerk to Justice Robert Jackson in 1953, he had written a memo arguing that racial segregation in public schools did not offend the Constitution. The future Justice Rehnquist explained that the memo had been written at Justice Jackson's request as an analytical exercise, and did not represent law clerk Rehnquist's views, either then or now. If the Senators had not accepted this explanation, such views could have provided ample grounds for refusing to place Justice Rehnquist on the Supreme Court. Some constitutional landmarks are so crucial to our sense of what America is all about that their dismantling should be considered off-limits, and candidates who would be at all likely to upend them should therefore be considered unfit.

Such outer boundaries exist on both ends of the traditional political spectrum, and may appropriately look a bit different to each member of the Senate. On *some* boundaries, though, *all* should be able to agree. For example, no one should be named to the Supreme Court who believes that the Bill of Rights should never have been applied to the states and who would, as a Justice, free state and local governments to act without regard to that charter of freedoms.

It has become fashionable in some quarters to take the position that the Bill of Rights was first "incorporated" into the Due Process Clause of the Fourteenth Amendment and applied to the states by the Warren Court, and that this recent "liberal" innovation can and should be undone when the nation moves into more conservative times. But long before Earl Warren and his brethren were appointed, the Supreme Court had required the states to respect many of the liberties enshrined in the Bill of Rights.

Even the ultraconservative Court of the early twentieth century, which struck down legislation that protected the rights of workers and of consumers, upheld rights of free speech and free exercise of religion against state infringement.

In *Meyer v. Nebraska*, the Supreme Court in 1923 invalidated a state law that prohibited foreign language instruction in private schools before the eighth grade. The law had been passed amid the tension of the nation's war with Kaiser Wilhelm's Germany, and was aimed at suppressing the culture and heritage of the state's German minority. If parents wish their children to learn German, the Court said, the state has no right to dictate otherwise, even if America is at war with Germany. Two years later, in the companion cases of *Pierce v. Society of Sisters* and *Pierce v. Hill Military Academy*, the Supreme Court declared unconstitutional a state law that required all children to attend *public* schools. The cardinal principle of these 1920s school cases is that the state has no power to "standardize its children" or foster a "homogeneous" people by completely foreclosing opportunities to be different. We saw how seriously the Supreme Court took this principle in the case of *West Virginia Board of Education v.*

Barnette in 1943, when it sided with freedom of conscience and belief in striking down the law that required all schoolchildren to salute the American flag.

It is possible that a nation which did not protect its citizens from state power in these ways could still be called civilized, but that approach misses the point. The question is not whether one could imagine a civilized society that would not recognize and protect a particular right, but whether that right is necessary in *our* regime of ordered liberty. In its opinion in *Meyer v. Nebraska*, the Supreme Court reviewed the methods that were used by the ancient Greeks and recommended by Plato to "submerge the individual and develop ideal citizens." As Justice McReynolds, in a rare display of tolerance, wrote for the Court, "Although such measures have been deliberately approved by men of great genius, their ideas touching the relation of the individual and the state were wholly different from those upon which our institutions rest; and it hardly will be affirmed that any legislature could impose such restrictions upon the people of a state without doing violence to both the letter and the spirit of the Constitution."

Our frame of reference is not some abstract notion of civilization or free government, but the *American* vision. Promises of freedom of speech and worship, guarantees of privacy of the home and the person, a ban on cruel and unusual punishment—these things are in the Bill of Rights because they define *our* aspirations, *our* idea of a just society. A nation in which state officials have the power to require prayers to a state-endorsed deity, to break into homes and "bug" telephones and bedrooms at will, or to amputate the hands of habitual shoplifters, might be a "civilized" society in some people's eyes, but it would not be America.

As another example, any judicial nominee who favored overturning the legislative apportionment cases and who denounced any role at all for the federal judiciary in preserving the fundamental democratic principle of "one person, one vote" would now be equally unsuitable as a Supreme Court Justice—and should be so regarded by all Senators even if the President were to disagree. And, to pick an illustration from the other end of the political continuum, no Senator should vote to confirm any candidate who believes that the Constitution's guarantees of equality before the law require the complete abolition of private property and contract. A communist notion of regimented social and economic equality is alien to our Constitution's pursuit of equality of opportunity. True, the demand that all Americans be accorded the equal protection of the laws has been held by the Supreme Court to require the government to make some efforts to put the rich and the poor on an equal footing. For example, the Court has struck down a variety of official fees that effectively locked the poor out of the courthouse or the voting booth. The Court has also struck down the traditional sentence of "thirty days or thirty dollars" when it led to the imprisonment of poor offenders solely for failure to pay the alternative fines that richer criminals could easily afford. But even if there is further movement by the Court in this direction—movement that I, among many, would welcome— any "reading" of the Constitution that treated the Equal Protection Clause as *completely* overwhelming the Constitution's explicit protections of property and contracts would be beyond the boundaries of acceptability. Although a nominee's endorsement of a constitutional amendment to this effect would pose no necessary barrier to confirmation, any candidate who favored reading the *existing* Constitution so "liberally" should not be confirmed.

Equally unfit for that high office would be candidates so committed to upholding a woman's right to terminate a pregnancy, or so determined to exclude official prayer from public schools, that they would strike down duly adopted constitutional amendments aimed at reversing the settled doctrine on these issues. Just as a nominee who would ignore a pro-choice amendment (if one were added to reinstate *Roe v. Wade* if and when that precedent is ever overruled) because of a right-to-life commitment must be rejected, so one who would simply ignore an anti-abortion amendment out of a pro-choice commitment is likewise unworthy of confirma-

tion. The Supreme Court's power and duty to say what
the Constitution *means* is subservient to the power to
amend that document through the machinery expressly
set forth in Article V of the Constitution itself.

The remaining wide range of political and constitutional opinion should constitute the field within which
the political branches necessarily maneuver in the appointment process. Both the President in nominating
candidates and Senators in deciding whether to confirm
them should determine the acceptable range of constitutional philosophy and should question potential Justices accordingly. Because the Senate has a veto power
but is not required to reach affirmative agreement on
an ideal candidate, there is no reason to insist that
individual Senators agree with one another, much less
that they agree with the President, on what an acceptable philosophy must include or exclude.

At the very least, though, we should be able to agree
that *a philosophy must be more than a bumper sticker*.
Knee-jerk attitudes, however sincerely held, about issues such as gun control, capital punishment, or the
right to life, are profoundly antithetical to the judicial
temperament. Litmus tests that seek out a candidate's
unswerving commitment to upholding or reversing a
particular legal precedent are simply not an acceptable
part of the appointment process. Indeed, appointing
"one-case" Justices makes even less sense than electing
"one-issue" political officers. The latter are also chosen
on a narrow and shortsighted basis, but at least they are
easily voted out of office in the next election after the
issue retreats into oblivion. One-case Justices, by contrast, are with the republic until death do us part—long
after the particular controversy is but a dim memory.

As Andrew Jackson's Treasury Secretary, Roger Taney
had followed the President's orders to sabotage Jackson's bête noire, the Bank of the United States. Passing over such renowned figures as Daniel Webster,
President Jackson twice nominated Taney to the Supreme Court so that Justice Taney could complete the
hatchet job on the Bank. As we have seen, the Senate
quashed the first nomination, but failed in an attempt

to block the second, so Taney became the nation's highest judicial officer. Twenty years after President Jackson left office, there were no Bank cases left to decide, but Chief Justice Taney was still around to author the infamous opinion in *Dred Scott v. Sandford*, which sanctified the status of blacks as property and made the Civil War all but inevitable. The plaudits that some legal scholars have accorded to Taney's tenure as Chief Justice cannot erase his leading role in the case that must rank as the greatest disaster—and greatest obscenity—in the history of the Court. Thus, if the President insists—unwisely and improperly—on nominating only those who express a politically approved view of a single issue, such as the "right to life" or school prayer, or only those who are found acceptable by a specific political or moral constituency, then each Senator has a special duty not to confirm. Such adherence to a specific presidential agenda reflects an unjudicious commitment not to a coherent constitutional philosophy, but to a slogan or even the outcome of a single case.

As a case study in the defects of litmus tests, consider *Roe v. Wade*, the 1973 decision that upheld a limited right for women to choose whether to have abortions—and the decision that is most often invoked as the focus of concern about how a Supreme Court nominee might vote in the future. It is perfectly appropriate to inquire into a judicial candidate's attitude toward *Roe*, and would in fact be bizarre *not* to, but the questions must address *principled* views about the decision and the legal doctrines relating to it—not mere aversion to, or mere endorsement of, its result. Regardless of *where* a nominee stands on an issue, a candidate for our highest court owes us an account of *why*. And that explanation must be based on principles and precedents, not prejudices or even good-faith preconceptions. There is nothing necessarily improper in an objection to *Roe v. Wade* based on a judgment that the Supreme Court gave insufficient weight to the value of fetal life, or on a protest that the Court gave too much deference to mainstream medical opinion. Nor is there any impropriety in an agreement with *Roe* based on a judgment that the contrary ruling would have given insufficient protection to women's rights or undue power to those who advocate a particular theory of personhood.

But nominees who would overrule *Roe* simply because they privately regard the fetus as a "person" and would defend all such persons regardless of the effect on a woman's rights, or because the Bill of Rights does not *explicitly* set forth a woman's substantive right to control her own body, should not receive a confirmation vote from any Senator who has regard for the Constitution as preserving a public system of private rights. Indeed, the Ninth Amendment to the Constitution makes it clear that the Bill of Rights is not, and "shall not be construed" as, an exhaustive and exclusive list of personal liberties. And several long lines of judicial decisions establish *some* right to privacy and autonomy in sexual matters. Thus, a nominee who would overturn *Roe v. Wade* should at least be prepared to explain why, in that nominee's view, those lines of cases do *not* properly converge on the result the Court reached in *Roe* or, if they do converge there, which of those lines the nominee would be likely to cut back— and how far.

Would the nominee, for example, overturn *Griswold v. Connecticut*, the case that struck down a state ban on the use of contraceptives? If not, how would the nominee justify overruling *Roe*? If the justification for making contraception a private choice while allowing states in their discretion to ban abortion is that each abortion takes a human life, then how would the nominee justify giving *states* the choice of which young lives to protect by law and which to leave to the mercy of private decision? Why, if the fetus is to be deemed a person, isn't a state ban on infanticide but not abortion a violation of the state's duty to protect all of humanity equally?

Indeed, a nominee who would reaffirm *Roe v. Wade* should be equally prepared to explain how that nominee reconciles a woman's liberty to end fetal life with the law's protection of *other* helpless human beings from what may seem to be equally justified destruction.

Does the nominee who would reaffirm *Roe* believe that fetal life is not entitled to be regarded as human? That, as the Supreme Court has asserted, the fetus is not a person—even in late pregnancy? If so, what is it that suddenly makes a newborn infant a "person"? Or might the nominee agree with *Roe* on the quite different ground that even if the unborn *are* persons, our laws do not generally compel adults, even parents, to sacrifice their bodies to keep others—even their own children—alive? Does the nominee support *Roe v. Wade* on the basis that—in a society that would not compel a mother or a father to donate a kidney, for example, in order to prevent a baby's death—it is fundamentally unfair to compel women, and women alone, to act as involuntary incubators for their infants? If so, then would the nominee at least be prepared to uphold laws evenhandedly requiring men and women *alike* to make significant bodily sacrifices for their unborn offspring, or laws requiring embryos slated for abortion to be transferred instead to artificial wombs, or to surrogate mothers, whenever technically feasible? Questions of this sort—about this issue and others—ought to be put to any prospective Justice, one who has expressed agreement with *Roe v. Wade* no less than one who has expressed misgivings about that landmark ruling.

From any Senator's perspective, one would suppose, those nominees who think that cases like *Roe v. Wade* are easy—either way—are of dubious fitness to serve as Supreme Court Justices. Cases like *Roe*, posing conflicts of important constitutional values, ought at least to be *recognized* as extremely difficult by any would-be Justice. The boundaries that mark off the acceptable range of views on such matters—the criteria that separate cases into the "hard" and the "easy"—will necessarily be drawn by the President and Senators according to their own considered constitutional views. But both branches owe a duty to the nation to satisfy themselves that a Supreme Court appointee's scale of constitutional values, on the full range of questions likely to come to the Court in the foreseeable future, represents a principled version of the value system envisioned by the Constitution.

It is by now obvious that Senators cannot intelligently fulfill their constitutional role in the appointment process without knowing where Supreme Court nominees stand on important precedents and issues. Probing questions must be asked, and responsive answers must be given. Previous Senates objected to Roger Taney's single-minded anti-federalism, to Harrold Carswell's segregationist views, and even to William Rehnquist's less extreme but still deeply troubling endorsement of sweeping government power to investigate citizens. Future Senates should take an equally assertive stance in reviewing future nominations to the Supreme Court.

THE NOMINEE'S BELIEFS ABOUT HOW A JUDGE MAKES A DECISION

A Supreme Court nominee's judicial philosophy is just as relevant a topic during confirmation hearings as are the nominee's views on the substance of the Constitution's commands. The Senate, like the President, should be vigorous in inquiring into a candidate's opinions about how the Justices should approach their labors. Even questions about a nominee's positions on doctrinal issues reveal something not only about those positions but also about his or her judicial temperament. For example, the Senate should hesitate to confirm a candidate who is unwilling to discuss in detail and in depth his or her approach to present and future constitutional controversies. The Supreme Court has room neither for Justices who are afraid to *defend* their ideas nor for those who *have* no ideas. After all, by the time of nomination, a would-be Justice ought to have opinions and convictions on the full range of topics of constitutional importance. A blank slate is not the sign of an open mind, but of an empty one—of immaturity and inexperience, and perhaps even of indifference.

Neither the President nor the Senate, however, should go so far as to seek from a nominee solemn promises or precise predictions on future votes. We have already seen that such litmus tests are a poor method of investigating a candidate's substantive constitutional philosophy. They are equally unsuitable for testing judicial temperament. During Justice O'Connor's confirmation hearings, for example, Senator Jeremiah Denton expressed his frustration in pinning her down on just how she would vote in future abortion cases. Her reluctance to make this sort of pat prediction was proper. As Justice O'Connor pointed out, no one can know in advance exactly how a particular issue will next present itself to the Supreme Court. Nominees should not be asked to travel forward in time to guess how an issue will next arise; Justices should decide cases on the basis of considered judgments made in full context, not of inflexible predispositions held in the abstract. The Constitution's prohibition of advisory opinions by the federal courts reflects this intuition that justice is best advanced by well-informed, concrete decisions, rather than by unbridled and purely hypothetical speculation.

If Senators and Presidents insist on knowing exactly how potential Justices will vote on specific cases in the future, rather than on probing candidates' views of broad constitutional issues, and if they nominate and confirm only those who give them the answers they want to hear, the Court will consist of two sorts of Justices, both profoundly ill-suited to the role. One variety of unworthy appointees will be lackeys who will promise anything and cynics who will say whatever the President or the Senators want to hear; these are people more interested in winning a Supreme Court seat than in pursuing with integrity a reasoned course of justice. The other category of bad choices will be appointees so dogmatic that the time travel entailed in predicting future votes is effortless; these are people who can know for certain and in advance exactly how they will vote in a given case because they act out of prejudice, not from reflective judgment.

Another important facet of judicial temperament is a candidate's understanding of the use of precedent—what the law calls the rule of *stare decisis:* literally, "to adhere to decided cases." The highest court in a land that claims to be governed by laws, not men, is no place for those who have no respect whatever for precedent and feel no obligation at all to link present decisions to those that have already become part of our history. Nominees who think that precedents are meaningless because it is purely an accident that one case reached the Court before another, for example, should receive no confirmation vote from any Senator with a belief that legal history, too, has its claims in a system of ordered liberty. By the same token, the Supreme Court of a nation that pays homage to principle rather than prejudice can have no room for judges who confine decisions that they dislike to their specific factual contexts, and who refuse to search such prior decisions for principles by which the case at hand should be decided. To ignore precedent simply out of distaste for where it points, or to pretend that a principle points nowhere simply because it is a principle with which one disagrees, is to forsake judicial analysis in favor of personal preference.

On the other hand, those candidates who would, for example, refuse even to consider modifying, say, *Roe v. Wade*, or perhaps the sterilization case, *Buck v. Bell*, simply *because* they are established precedents, are equally unsuited for a seat on the Supreme Court, and should be voted down by any Senator who views constitutional principles as subject to reexamination when circumstances so require. Justices who look upon precedents as divine edicts inscribed on stone tablets lack a sufficient appreciation of the evolutionary nature of constitutional law. It is sometimes more important that the Court be right than that it be consistent.

For most of us, the proper role of precedent in constitutional adjudication will be found at the end of a middle road. The nation needs and deserves to have a steady hand at the Constitution's wheel, but the Supreme Court occasionally must overrule its earlier cases because legislative correction of a *constitutional* decision is all but impossible. An amendment to the great charter itself is usually necessary, and such a phenomenon is rare indeed; in the Court's entire history, only four decisions have been reversed by constitutional amendment. In 1798 the Eleventh Amendment, which protected the states from citizen suits brought in federal court without congressional authority, reversed the Court's 1793 decision in *Chisholm v. Georgia*. The previously discussed decision in *Dred Scott v. Sandford*, handed down in 1857, was overturned by the Thirteenth Amendment in 1865, which outlawed slavery, and the Fourteenth Amendment in 1868, which declared that all Americans, native-born or naturalized, are full citizens and entitled to the equal protection of the laws. The Supreme Court declared the federal income tax unconstitutional by a 5-4 vote in *Pollock v. Farmers' Loan & Trust Co.* in 1895, but that decision was nullified by the Sixteenth Amendment in 1913. Finally, in the 1970 case of *Oregon v. Mitchell*, the Court invalidated, again by a margin of one Justice, an act of Congress that gave eighteen-year-olds the right to vote in state, as well as federal, elections. Congress, with prompt ratification by the states, quickly returned the gesture just one year later: the Twenty-sixth Amendment voided the Court's holding.

Even when a decision involves solely the interpretation of a congressional statute and thus can be overruled by "mere" legislation, the task is often daunting, for a national legislative consensus is often brief, and there is no assurance that Congress will be able to find the common ground a second time. Since there is no effective appeal from the decisions of the Supreme Court, that tribunal itself must constantly reassess the positions it takes. As Justice Brandeis once wrote, "The Court bows to the lessons of experience and the force of better reasoning, recognizing that the process of trial and error, so fruitful in the physical sciences, is appropriate also in the judicial function."

Perhaps the most important qualification for being a Supreme Court Justice is the possession of an open mind. Even Oliver Cromwell, the seventeenth-century English revolutionary who is remembered for his self-righteous religious zeal, once advised, "Brethren, by the bowels of Christ I beseech you, bethink you that you may be mistaken."

THE NOMINEE'S VIEW OF THE SUPREME COURT'S ROLE

Inquiry into a candidate's judicial philosophy and beliefs as to the proper role of the third branch of government is certainly legitimate, but serves little purpose if conducted in terms of shibboleths like "judicial activism" or "restraint," "liberal" or "conservative." The "liberal" Warren Court was an "activist" tribunal according to the conventional wisdom, but the "conservative" Burger Court, despite frequent lip service to the notion, has itself shown little restraint. In the last decade or so the Court has written sweeping decisions striking down Congress's organization of the bankruptcy courts, invalidating comprehensive campaign finance reform, and voiding nearly all regulation of abortion. The Burger Court has in fact struck down far more legislation than the Warren Court, and in fewer years. *Immigration & Naturalization Service v. Chadha* presented a challenge to the "legislative veto," a technique in which Congress delegated power to the executive branch but reserved for itself—or even for just the House or the Senate alone—a right to veto particular exercises of that power. When the Burger Court declared the legislative veto a violation of the Constitution's separation of powers in 1983, it invalidated with a single stroke more federal statutory provisions than the Supreme Court had struck down in the preceding two centuries.

The difference between the two Courts—and a more promising area of questioning for the Senate to pursue—is the *nature* and *direction* of their activism. The Warren Court had an agenda for legal change, and was willing to make fundamental choices when necessary—all in the service of "due process," "freedom of speech," and "equal protection of the laws." The more recent activism of the Burger Court is both more pragmatic, and more mechanical, seemingly guided not by a substantive vision of a humane future but by a desire to moderate social conflict through compromise and accommodation; the Burger Court does not *assert* constitutional values so much as *adjust* them. It is, therefore, more revealing to ask potential Justices about the substantive *directions* they believe the Supreme Court should take, and why—and how they would have it proceed along those paths—than to ask whether they would assign themselves opaque and usually self-serving labels like "judicial activist" or "judicial conservative."

Does the nominee believe that the increasing complexity and danger of our world require giving the President more discretionary power? Or does the growth of government's authority require even more vigilance and more suspicion of the executive branch on behalf of the Bill of Rights? Does the nominee believe that the Court should advance the Constitution's values by confident proclamations of principles beyond price, such as government's duty to obey its own laws? Or instead that the Court should, in the main, refine those principles by balancing competing considerations and weighing the relative costs and benefits of enforcing each principle to its logical limits? Does the nominee seek to implement a unifying vision of constitutional law? Or prefer to take things purely case by case, and change the law only in the increments that come with fine-spun distinctions? Does the nominee look seriously to the lessons of the past and the challenges of the future, or only to the exigencies and political mood of the moment?

Although some may be alarmed by the way that Justices with a mission might stride over the law's established cases and classifications, there may be an even more disturbing danger in the method of those Justices who claim to take just one small step at a time. If your eyes are set on a destination, you can see—and others can criticize—where you are heading. But if you look only at your feet, the better to supervise each little step, you may easily stray far from your original path—and may do so in a way that is too slow and too gradual to be noticed by the citizens who have entrusted you with the power to construe their Constitution.

Chapter Seven

PRESERVING THE OVERALL BALANCE: TESTING NOMINEES IN CONTEXT

There is a second lens through which any prospective Supreme Court appointee should be viewed. Even if a particular nominee is qualified and falls within all the limits so far suggested, we must ask how confirmation of the individual Justice would affect the *overall balance* of the Court. This shift in focus may mean that nominees who fall *within* the President's and a given Senator's circles of acceptability, when considered on their own merits, will fall *outside* the tighter circle drawn by a Senator when considering the context of the nominee's appointment. This is the way it has, at times, been— and the way it should be.

On one level, this concern for balance should remind us that the current Supreme Court is overwhelmingly white, male, and Protestant. At various times in its history, the diversity of the Supreme Court was enhanced through such customs as a "New York seat" (from 1806 to 1894), a "New England seat" (1789 to 1932), a "Jewish seat" 1916 to 1970), or a "Catholic seat" (1894 to 1949, and 1956 to the present). Obviously, mere tokenism is not a serious policy to pursue in Supreme Court appointments, and these appointment traditions could never by themselves create the kind of diverse and finely poised Court that the republic needs. But given the long tradition of conscious attention to geographic and religious diversity on the Court, the promotion of increased diversity with respect to gender and race is certainly a legitimate value to keep in mind.

On a more probing level, the President, the Senate, and individual Senators should consider what impact a particular appointment would have in the context of the distribution of judicial inclinations that characterizes the Court at the time that appointment is made. One important aim, although too few Presidents have actively pursued it, should be to produce a healthy mix of competing views. To use the standard, if often misleading labels, a Court that includes five "liberal" Justices, two "conservatives," and one "moderate" at its center, could be dangerously imbalanced by another "liberal" appointment, while a bench comprising four "conservatives," three "moderates," and a single "liberal" already tilts too far in the opposite direction and could be righted only by the addition of another "liberal." A Supreme Court with three or four Justices of both the "liberal" and "conservative" persuasions and a pair of vacancies to be filled presents a prime opportunity for the addition of two centrists to provide "swing" votes as checks upon extremes at both ends of the spectrum. The Senate's ideal role is as a ballast—to adjust the drift of the Supreme Court as represented by a given appointment.

Such concern for diversity and balance certainly does not justify a Senate refusal to confirm a nominee to whom the Senators' only objection is that the candidate would not have been *their* first or even second choice. In Supreme Court appointments the Constitution allows only the President his "druthers." Allowing each Senator to confirm solely from the Senator's own "short list" would prescribe paralysis in the Supreme Court appointment process. But if the appointment of a particular nominee would push the Court in a substantive direction that a Senator conscientiously deems undesirable because it would upset the Court's equilibrium or exacerbate what he views as an already excessive conservative *or* liberal bias, then that Senator can and should vote against confirmation. To vote otherwise would be to abdicate a solemn trust.

There is one seeming paradox in the idea of voting against an otherwise qualified nominee solely on the basis of the effect the appointment would have on the Court's overall equilibrium and direction: such a vote makes a nominee's confirmation turn not only on the potential Justice's intrinsic merit and suitability for a seat on the Supreme Court, but also on the specific vacancy being filled, the impact of previous appointments, and the configuration and inclination of those who still serve on the Court at the time of the appointment. For example, when Peter Daniel was nominated by President Martin Van Buren in 1841, the Court already had a pronounced anti-federal bias resulting from Van Buren's previous appointment of John McKinley, and from five Jackson appointments. When considered alone, Daniel, a respected politician and experienced federal judge, was an acceptable candidate; but in 1841 the Supreme Court needed greater breadth of political disposition, not another intensely partisan Jacksonian Democrat. The Court Van Buren and Jackson left behind them was too doctrinaire to contend with the threat to the Union created by the increasing separatism of the Southern states—a separatism fueled by the Court's own promotion of states' rights. So Daniel should have been rejected.

Considering judicial nominations in context can just as easily make a particular candidate even more—rather than less—attractive. The Court from which Justice William O. Douglas retired in 1975 was in some ways in need of a new center of gravity. The Court had been highly progressive on the civil liberties front during the years Earl Warren was Chief Justice, and had also handed down decisions that revolutionized the rights of the accused. With the appointment of Chief Justice Warren Burger and three other Justices by President Nixon, the Court lurched in the opposite direction and retrenched on those recently recognized liberties. President Gerald Ford's nomination of Judge John Paul Stevens to replace Douglas was a nicely balanced act of statesmanship. Stevens was a sound choice on his own merits; he was a respected expert in antitrust law, and in his five years on a federal appellate court he had earned a reputation as an open-minded judge. When evaluated in the context of the Burger Court to which he was nominated, Justice Stevens became an even more suitable choice, for the ideologically divided Court was in need of a moderate jurist who defies traditional categories. While he has usually operated at the Court's center, Justice Stevens often writes separate concurring opinions that reach the same results by routes different from those taken by the majority, and he has been a vigorous voice in dissent from the opinions of the Nixon appointees when he believes that they side too much with government against those accused of crime.

If this contextual approach to appointment appears complex and difficult for a Senator to apply, we must remember that no one promised that the confirmation process would be any easier than other senatorial duties. If the contextual approach seems unfair to the nominee, we must remember that the Senate is not reviewing the qualifications of nominees in order to award them yet more framed certificates to hang on their office walls. A Supreme Court seat is not a merit badge, no matter how meritorious a nominee may be when his or her qualifications are assessed in artificial isolation. What is at stake, after all, is the composition of the highest court in the land and the future of the Constitution—a future that we have seen powerfully shaped by individual Justices. Senators would be gravely remiss in their duty to the nation if they supported appointments that would force the Supreme Court to veer off onto—or, indeed, to remain stuck on—what the Senators themselves perceive as a constitutionally dangerous course simply because they could not bring themselves to think hard about the Constitution, to hurt a nominee's feelings, or to deny the President his fondest wish.

One possible objection to this emphasis on balance is the proposition that the Supreme Court ought to be kept in step with the times; shifts in the national temperament—be they progressive or conservative, libertarian or authoritarian—*ought* to change the kinds of

Justices we appoint. But such an argument profoundly misconceives the role of the Supreme Court in our tripartite system of government. The Court should not merely reflect the spirit of the times; that is the proper role of the political branches. If the Court becomes merely a snapshot of the presently predominant social and political philosophies, it is doomed by the regime of life tenure to become an anachronism.

One might think that a well-balanced Supreme Court bench would be a natural product of the appointment system, since the Justices are replaced one at a time, and since the Court is a collage that comprises and collects, at any given moment, the choices of several Presidents. But, as we have seen, the great majority of the Justices who have served on the Court since its creation were appointed in the same year as another Justice. It is far from uncommon for a plurality or even a majority of the members of the Court to be the result of a single President's nominations. Then, too, even Supreme Courts whose composition is the work of several presidential hands can be remarkably uniform in outlook. Since it takes only five Justices to make a majority, Supreme Courts of varied origin have given us decisions that are remarkably monolithic.

In 1905, early in the Supreme Court's period of hostility toward socioeconomic legislation directed at correcting market failures, the Court consisted of Justices appointed by no fewer than six different Presidents. Those Chief Executives were a diverse group, ranging from Rutherford B. Hayes to Theodore Roosevelt to Grover Cleveland. Thirty-one years later, the *Lochner* era was still in full swing, with the Court striking down minimum wage laws and New Deal legislation with apparent abandon. Yet the membership of the Court had been completely transformed; it now consisted of Justices appointed by five Presidents as different from one another as Herbert Hoover, Calvin Coolidge, and Woodrow Wilson. In 1965, in the heyday of the Warren Court, the nine Justices owed their nominations to four Presidents, including F.D.R., Dwight Eisenhower, and John Kennedy. The 1973 Court that

decided the abortion case, *Roe v. Wade*, was the work
of five Presidents—three Democrats and two Republicans. The Supreme Court as of early 1985, hardly a
model of diversified balance, nevertheless owes its members' appointments to six Presidents as unlike one another in their political outlooks as John Kennedy, Gerald
Ford, and Ronald Reagan.

Thus it is clear that the mechanics of presidential
nomination, individual Senate confirmation, and life tenure cannot by themselves assure a balanced Supreme
Court. It is the responsibility of the President and the
Senate to reassess the diversity of outlook represented
on the Court each time a vacancy occurs. The trajectory
of the Court's recent decisions should be charted, and
the parameters of acceptability discussed in the preceding chapter should be adjusted accordingly, to make
certain that the new appointment will not tend to push
the Court too far off course, in any direction.

What constitutes a desirable path for the Supreme
Court is, of course, open to debate—and should be
debated. The fact that the Constitution puts the power
of appointment jointly into the hands of both the President and the Senate, for reasons examined more closely
in the next chapter, suggests that each political branch
ought to act as a balance for the pull asserted by the
other.

In discussing judicial appointments in the context of
the future direction of the Supreme Court, the shorthand labels "left" and "right," "liberal" and "conservative," are too blunt to be of much value. Although the
problem of Supreme Court equilibrium is of enduring
significance, to understand its dynamics we must get
down to cases. The Supreme Court as composed in
early 1985 provides a rich source of material to illustrate this book's perspectives, even though the Courts
to which this book's basic lessons might be applied in
the 1990s and beyond may well look very different
indeed, and may pose problems of context quite unlike
those of the present era. For purposes of illustration,
though, the present Court will have to do. On too many
occasions, as it happens, the present Supreme Court

has narrowly skirted perilous cliffs; these examples reinforce the lesson that careless and unexamined appointments could all too easily push the Court over the
edge. It is a lesson whose relevance is timeless, even if
the present occasion for learning it will pass.

IS THIS COURT WORTH SAVING?

Before trying to gauge the effect that a given appointment will have on the Supreme Court's balance, we
must consider whether the balance struck by previous
appointments is one worth saving. As of 1985, the answer to this question, even from the perspective of
someone who has usually been a critic of the Burger
Court, is a resounding yes. It is true that the present
Court has displayed some troubling tendencies and made
many disturbing decisions. It has often been insensitive
to the rights of prisoners and criminal defendants; it has
been too deferential to executive and bureaucratic authority; it has been unenthusiastic in defense of rights
of free expression where the poor and discontented are
concerned; it has devalued the government's moral and
legal obligation to obey the Constitution in the course
of law enforcement; and it has manifested a fascination
with pseudo-economic modes of analysis that resolve
questions of constitutional principle by calculating costs
and benefits and computing marginal effects.

Yet, for all this, the Burger Court certainly has not
given away all of the hard-won liberties of the past, and
there is much to applaud in its jurisprudence. It has
maintained the struggle for racial equality, even going
so far as to uphold some government and private efforts
to remedy the impact of past discrimination through
affirmative action. It has been the first Supreme Court
in history to champion the rights of the press and the
public to attend criminal trials, so that citizens may
observe firsthand the way in which the government
conducts its most direct confrontations with those it
governs. The Burger Court also deserves credit for
extending the Constitution's protection to those who

are mentally impaired. In a series of unanimous decisions, the Court has promoted both the dignity and the liberty of an often forgotten group of citizens. States may not confine the mentally ill solely to keep them out of sight. And even if the state wishes to provide treatment for the mentally ill rather than merely to put them in storage, it may not involuntarily commit them to mental institutions without due process of law. Finally, we must not forget that more than half of all Americans—those who are women—now enjoy the right to "equal protection of the laws" because a majority of the Burger Court has declared that government may not discriminate on the basis of gender.

FREEDOM OF SPEECH AND OF THE PRESS

Since the birth of the republic the press has been accorded a special role. In times of national crisis, such as the Watergate affair, the news media have risen in status almost to the level of a fourth branch of government. The Burger Court has not always shared this view of the press. It has declined to provide special protection for news sources and informants and has allowed police to search newsrooms for evidence of criminal activity by third parties. The press currently enjoys no special freedom under the First Amendment from the obligation of citizens generally to respond to subpoenas and other judicial demands for information, however great might be the resulting impediment to news gathering from sources wary of disclosure. In an age when hundreds of millions of people depend upon the media as their sole source of information, this lack of sympathy for the notion that the press has a special "right" to gather news may not bode well for the future of the informed citizenry that James Madison considered essential to the political health of the republic.

The Burger Court, however, has left the news media with rights of access to information at least *equal* to those of the general public. For example, the press, like the public, now has a constitutionally based right to observe trials—a right that the Burger Court deserves great credit for proclaiming, and then extending, in a series of landmark rulings beginning with *Richmond Newspapers v. Virginia* in 1980. And the Burger Court has maintained a stalwart intolerance for "gag orders" and other prior restraints on publication. Thus, in its 1971 decision in the *Pentagon Papers Case,* the Court denied the federal government the power to block publication of confidential Defense Department documents about the Vietnam War by the *New York Times* and the *Washington Post.* The Justices would permit the government to stop the presses only if it could demonstrate a substantial certainty of grave harm to national security. Similarly, in *Nebraska Press Association v. Stuart* five years later, the Burger Court reversed a trial judge's order that barred coverage of a criminal trial because the trial court's conclusion that publicity would infringe the defendant's right to a fair trial was "speculative." Backing up this ban on prepublication restraints is the Supreme Court's consistent holding that newspapers may not be punished after the fact for printing information that was legally obtained. Once the cat is out of the bag, the Supreme Court will rarely help the government recapture it. Finally, in a move reminiscent of the aversion the Founding Fathers felt toward the Stamp Act, the Burger Court conceded at least some degree of favored status for the press when the Court in 1983 struck down a tax on ink that burdened only newspapers.

The Supreme Court has always had difficulty in First Amendment cases in deciding where "speech" ends and "conduct" begins. For example, the Court has allowed Congress a largely free hand in regulating labor union picketing, declaring that such expressive activity is not speech but "speech plus," and is therefore entitled to only the most limited First Amendment protection. Nevertheless, in *NAACP v. Claiborne Hardware Co.* in 1982, the Burger Court unanimously held that a peaceful boycott by black citizens of businesses run by whites was protected by the First Amendment because its purpose was to secure compliance by both civic and business leaders with demands for equality and racial justice. Still, the Burger Court of late has often taken, in Justice Stewart's words, a "crabbed view" of the First Amendment. In *Clark v. Community for Creative Non-Violence* in 1984, for example, the Court upheld a Park Service rule that allowed those concerned with the plight of the homeless to erect tent villages in the parks near the White House, but denied the demonstrators the right actually to *fall asleep* in their tents. The Court evidently failed to see how the rule thus robbed the demonstration of its expressive punch.

The Burger Court's distaste for symbolic speech is part of a general retreat to the view that only verbal communication on matters of clear public import is worthy of full constitutional protection. For many, that represents an unacceptably narrow conception of *why* the Constitution protects free speech in the first place, and entails a dangerous delegation to the courts of power to decide *which* "speech" counts as sufficiently "political" to merit undiluted defense in the Constitution's name. Who among us would be satisfied to have judges—or, for that matter, other officials—decide whether Orwell's *1984* is a futuristic novel or a political tract? Whether Fierstein's *Torch Song Trilogy* is a gripping play or a manifesto of gay liberation? Whether a peace symbol is a statement of belief or merely a circle marked with lines? The appointment of a Justice who believes that the First Amendment guards only verbal political expression could well propel the Court over the cliff on which it is precariously perched.

The present Court also gives evidence of viewing freedom of speech as just another competing social interest to be weighed on the Constitution's scales, rather than as a heavy "thumb" that the Bill of Rights itself places on the side of a robust and uninhibited flow of information and ideas. For example, the Constitution has long been interpreted to provide the privilege of criticizing the government. But when free expression conflicts even marginally with government assertions of "national security interests," the contemporary Burger Court has shown a disturbing willingness to reverse that privilege.

Finally, the Burger Court has trouble with the fact that our understanding of the First Amendment must evolve to meet the stresses of new communication technologies. Thus the Court continues to apply a rigid distinction between the print and electronic media in an age when the two are merging and may soon be indistinguishable. The "equal-time rule" that requires television and radio stations to give citizens and political candidates a chance to respond to their opponents was upheld by the Court on the theory that opportunities for such electronic mass communication were scarce; since the radio and television broadcast frequencies can accommodate only so many stations, the government must regulate them and license broadcasters. If the government did not require those broadcasters to give opposing viewpoints equal time, some speakers would be cut off from this most potent of the mass media. Newspapers do not have a similar obligation to provide space in their columns for opposing views or speakers, on the theory that there is no limit on the number of newspapers in the market; anyone can set up a printing press.

But technological advances have made possible a host of new radio and TV channels, both on the airwaves and on cables. Meanwhile, the economics of newspaper publishing and the growth of nationwide chain papers have radically altered the print medium. Since many cities now have only one daily newspaper but three or more TV stations and dozens of radio stations, the premise underlying the equal-time rule has been wholly reversed. And the rapid development of home computers hooked up to media of all sorts raises serious questions about how particular media are even to be *classified* for legal purposes when technological worlds collide. The appointment of nominees who would adhere mechanically to an outmoded dichotomy between the electronic and print media could leave the Court in an even poorer state of readiness for contending with the Information Age.

RACIAL DISCRIMINATION

The present Supreme Court has not been as firmly committed as the Warren Court to racial equality before the law. It has evinced a growing dissatisfaction with politically unpopular means of integrating schools, and has limited the power of government to compel choices that would redress the effects of past discrimination through affirmative action. The Burger Court maintains that mere disproportionate impact on blacks is not enough to invalidate a government hiring standard, a local zoning ordinance, or the structure of a city's electoral districts; before the courts step in, there must be a showing of *intentional* discrimination.

In all fairness, though, the Burger Court has in some respects had a tougher job than its predecessor. The Warren Court confronted egregious forms of apartheid and overt racial subjugation. It could with relative ease identify the "bad guys" among the school boards and legislatures. To a large degree the work of the Warren Court in the field of racial justice was a success. As a result, the Burger Court has had to contend with more subtle forms of racism and the myriad ways in which the legacy of past discrimination has become engrained in our society and economy. Delving into the heart of a society to correct the subtle structures that perpetuate racial disadvantage requires a more delicate touch than that used in simply cutting off a practice like school segregation, and the Burger Court has not always been a willing surgeon. For example, the Court has endorsed affirmative action programs in employment where those minority members who are helped can show that they are the direct victims of previous discrimination by the employer. But many of the Justices blanch at the burden affirmative action plans sometimes impose on those members of the majority—usually white males—who are passed over in order to accommodate the minority group. If future appointments to the Supreme Court add Justices too fearful of the practical difficulties and too obsessed with the individual costs that the quest for racial equality often entails, the Court's basic commitment to the principles from which that quest springs could be in serious jeopardy.

SEX DISCRIMINATION

Even if the constitutional guarantee of equal protection of the laws has not been deployed with overwhelming vigor by the Burger Court in the area of race, all must acknowledge its historic role in securing the constitutional right of equality for women. As late as 1961, it was the *Warren* Court that held it proper to exclude women from jury service because they were the "center of home and family life." The first decisions upholding equal rights for women came out of the *Burger* Court, beginning in 1971, and for the next decade a majority of the Justices repeatedly attacked the archaic stereotypes of the past. Laws that assume that all women are housewives who play no part in the financial support of their families, and that give husbands sole control over family property, have earned the present Court's emphatic rejection. The Court has facilitated women's access to traditionally male jobs, and has even held that a woman has a statutory right to sue her law firm for denying her a partnership on the basis of her gender. And, of course, the Burger Court's troubling and controversial abortion decisions have pioneered women's rights of choice and autonomy.

For many, however, the Burger Court's pathbreaking work in rooting out sex discrimination has not gone far enough. In 1981 the Court upheld the male-only military registration law without requiring the government to prove the necessity of such discrimination both against men, who are alone subjected to this burden, *and* women, who are alone denied an equal role in national defense and an equal share in the benefits of veterans. A more general flaw is the Burger Court's willingness automatically to treat what it sees as the "natural" differences between men and women—such as pregnancy and women's vulnerability to rape—as legitimate reasons for denying women equal opportunity in employment. The Court can do more than merely refuse to magnify and exaggerate real differences between men and women. It might also take account of social reality and see in the Constitution a purpose to combat affirmatively the inequities that result when the law invokes even genuine biological differences to justify the imposition of legal disadvantages. The Burger Court's place in history as a pioneer in equal protection for women may be secure, but if the rights won by women in those innovative decisions are to be equally secure, future appointments to the Court must be made with special care. The positive legacy of the Burger Court could easily be squandered by the appointment of more Justices who think it "natural" that the law automatically translates the presence of a second X-chromosome into rules and institutions that make women second-class citizens.

INSENSITIVITY TO LEGISLATIVE ATTEMPTS TO PROMOTE EQUALITY

On occasion the Burger Court has not simply reneged on the Constitution's promises of equality; it has gone further and has even frustrated carefully considered legislative efforts to correct inequalities in the distribution of wealth and power. In the crucial field of campaign finance the Supreme Court, in the 1976 case of *Buckley v. Valeo*, struck down major parts of Congress's comprehensive reform plan—a plan aimed at reducing the overwhelming influence of money in political campaigns so that smaller, less well-financed voices might be heard. In an unapologetic affirmation of the adage "Money talks," the Court held that financial contributions to candidates and causes, and expenditures made by the parties in a political contest, are forms of expression fully protected by the First Amendment. Some limits on campaign contributions were upheld as constitutional, but the Court held in 1976—and reaffirmed in 1985—that Congress could impose no limit on the amounts spent by candidates for office or by committees independently advancing a cause or a candidacy. Elections thus remain as much battles of private budgets as contests of ideas.

In 1978 the Burger Court held, in effect, that corporations—as artificial legal "persons"—have the same First Amendment rights as the rest of us. Therefore, in *First National Bank of Boston v. Bellotti,* the Court struck down a state's attempt to reduce the power of loud corporate voices to drown out the competing views of regular citizens. The Court's vision of freedom of expression focuses on speech in the abstract; it includes little sympathy for legislative efforts to correct some of the concrete distributional failures in the marketplace of ideas—failures that allow the wealthy to flood the market with their views and crowd out the expression of ideas that are not as amply funded.

In the same spirit, the Supreme Court in 1978 overturned a Minnesota law that protected the pension rights of workers in the event that their employers decided to shut down the factories in which they toiled. Although it engaged in a lengthy and complicated analysis of the pension protection statute, in essence the Court told Minnesota that it was not free under the Constitution to favor the economic interests of workers over those of their employers. In contrast to this rigorous judicial scrutiny of a state law that *protected* pension rights, two years later the Court applied a much more lenient standard of review in upholding a federal law that *terminated* the vested pension rights of some railroad workers. The analysis employed by the Court in these cases was highly technical and more than a little arbitrary. But the way the cases came out makes it hard to avoid the sense that, for the Burger Court, the Constitution protects most vigorously the economic rights of those who have the greatest economic and political clout. The appointment of additional Justices who insist on imposing on the legislature *their* notions of desirable remedial legislation could only make the present situation worse.

DEFERENCE TO THE EXECUTIVE

In recent years the Burger Court has shown a distressing tendency to side with the President in resolving controversies over the separation of powers. Recall that, in 1983, the Court declared unconstitutional the widely employed legislative veto—which, as we saw, had been the major device by which the House and Senate have attempted over the past half century to maintain meaningful oversight of executive power in an ever-expanding regulatory state. Without the legislative veto, Congress enjoys considerably reduced power to prevent the executive branch from abusing the authority delegated to it by Congress. But to a Court more worried about preserving presidential prerogatives than about rectifying such imbalances, that objection counts for little.

The expansion of presidential power not only disrupts the balance among the three branches of government; it also has consequences for individual liberty. In 1984 the Court upheld, by a 5–4 vote, the President's power to ban tourist travel to Cuba, despite a well-established constitutional rule that a citizen's right to travel abroad may not be curtailed without a clear authorization from Congress. The four dissenting Justices convincingly argued that Congress had not given the President free rein to restrict foreign travel by Americans; indeed, Congress had expressly limited the President's discretion. But a majority of the Supreme Court was willing to ignore those limitations. A Court that consistently interprets congressional delegations of executive power so broadly, while construing congressional limitations on that same power narrowly or invalidating them altogether, will soon leave the Constitution's system of checks and balances in a precarious state. The appointment of even one additional Justice inclined to defer to the President would take us a giant stride closer to the reality of an imperial presidency.

Observing that the "Court increasingly acts as the adjunct" of prosecutors and executives "irrespective of the Constitution's fundamental guarantees," Justices Brennan and Marshall concluded a dissenting opinion early in 1985 with the "hope that this day too will soon pass." Will it? Or will it lead to an even darker night for basic freedom? The answer will depend on the choice of future Justices for our nation's highest court.

ABDICATION TO PROFESSIONAL "EXPERTISE"

The Court's deferential endorsement of the expertise of the executive branch is only part of its general trend toward granting bureaucrats and professionals ever-increasing power over our lives and liberties—which is hardly a conservative notion. In the 1984 pair of prison cases discussed earlier—*Hudson v. Palmer* and *Block v. Rutherford*—the Supreme Court ruled, 5 to 4, that the claims of efficient penal administration outweighed the rights of prisoners, including those who were awaiting trial and thus still presumed innocent, to any privacy or shred of dignity. It was there that the Court deferred to the power of prison officials to confiscate and destroy all of a prisoner's personal papers, from a letter from his wife to a photograph of his child, and to forbid, even without a showing of any threat to prison safety, all physical contact with visiting family members, including a prisoner's infant daughter.

"Experts" in other fields have been accorded the same sort of freedom from meaningful judicial review. Public school teachers may discipline schoolchildren with beatings without first providing any notice to the child's parents or any sort of a hearing or an explanation. They may search students without judicial warrants and on less than "probable cause." Minors may be involuntarily committed to mental institutions on the authority of psychiatrists without any sort of hearing or the approval of any court or other government agency. And, perhaps most significantly, the Court has seen fit to leave the question of abortion largely in the hands of the medical profession. The landmark 1973 ruling in *Roe v. Wade* can certainly be defended as protecting a woman's right to reproductive autonomy. But it is not always noticed that the Burger Court instead cast the abortion decision in terms of the fetus's medical "viability," concluding that a doctor, acting at a woman's request, may opt for abortion until the time the fetus can survive outside the womb, and that the state may all but ban the procedure thereafter. In so ruling, the Court relied heavily on a consensus of medical expertise to resolve the constitutional issues, and expressed its holding largely in the language of a physician's right, as a medical professional, to prescribe treatment for "his" patient.

As both public and private bureaucracies expand and as more trades and occupations assume the status of professions, the Supreme Court's ready deference to professional "specialists" will become more and more troubling, and the need for Justices who are undaunted by claims of technical expertise will become ever more acute.

CONSTITUTIONAL COST-BENEFIT ANALYSIS

A corollary of the Supreme Court's enthusiasm for "expert" resolution of all sorts of problems is its newfound fondness for the tools of the systems analyst: cost-benefit comparisons and assessments of marginal effects. These techniques are rarely appropriate when dealing with constitutional principles rather than with engineering designs or with business judgments. Yet, in the 1980s, the Court began to apply such techniques with growing frequency to the Bill of Rights itself.

The Fifth Amendment, for instance, promises that no one will be convicted and sent to jail on the basis of coerced testimony. Whatever the "costs" or "benefits" might be, that solemn promise is broken whenever a judge admits into evidence confessions extracted by the police before the suspect has been informed that he has a right to remain silent and a right to obtain the help of a lawyer. Similarly, the Fourth Amendment promises that all of us will be secure from unreasonable searches. This security is breached whenever a judge allows into the courtroom evidence seized by the police in an illegal search. Yet in the *Leon* case, as we have seen, the Supreme Court decided that the "benefits" of excluding evidence are negligible when it has been obtained illegally but in good faith, or—as was the situation in a related case called *New York v. Quarles*—by coercion, but in the interest of public safety. The Court calculated that the unlawful police conduct in such cases was reasonable and therefore not likely to be deterred by the threat of exclusion from the courtroom. To the Court, the tangible "costs" of enforcing the Fourth and Fifth Amendments in these cases—the unpleasant sight of a criminal going unpunished just because the government did not follow its own rules—exceeded the nebulous and largely philosophical "benefits" of vindicating the Constitution's guarantees. By the Supreme Court's computation, the Bill of Rights simply could not, in the Court's own words, "pay its way." The apparent willingness of the Burger Court to sacrifice basic constitutional principles to expediency suggests a troublesome indifference to the fact that basic personal liberties are neither rooted in the law of averages nor assigned on the basis of efficiency.

But the Court has by no means allowed expediency to crowd out *all* concern for constitutional rights. Evidently misled into the contrary view by the Court's pattern of pro-police rulings, the State of Louisiana tried to convince the Justices in late 1984 that police should be allowed to search the home of a murder suspect without a warrant simply because the suspect, who had tried to commit suicide after shooting her husband in their home, was unconscious at the time of the search and thus had a "diminished expectation of privacy." The state even sought to rely on the somewhat mystical theory that the victim, who lay dead on the premises, would welcome the search of what had been his home if only he were able to speak. But the Supreme Court unanimously rejected the state's occult arguments and summarily reversed the murder conviction in an unsigned opinion issued without even setting the case for the usual oral presentation.

Less than two weeks later, the Court, this time by a

vote of 6 to 3, summarily reversed the position of
Illinois that an eighteen-year-old suspect, held in custody by detectives in a police interrogation room, could
continue to be questioned even after requesting the
assistance of counsel. The Illinois authorities had argued that the suspect's request for a lawyer was fatally
ambiguous—evidently because his request was punctuated with the word "uh." Although three Justices
unfortunately accepted Illinois's position, the six remaining Justices had no difficulty rejecting it. Thus a
majority of the Court affirmed the principle that citizens retain their civil rights even when they fail to
assert them in the Queen's English.

The upshot is that, in sufficiently clear cases of illegal
search and seizure or unlawful interrogation, the Burger
Court continues to enforce Warren Court protections
for ordinary citizens suspected of crime—protections
that a more authoritarian Court, one as prepared to defer
to claims of police power as were the courts of Louisiana and Illinois, might well cease to take seriously.

ABUSE OF JUDICIAL TECHNICALITIES

Traditionally, access to the federal courts to sue when
one has been injured has been limited by a host of often
arcane requirements that go by such names as "standing," "ripeness," and "justiciability." The present Supreme Court has a tendency to manipulate these technical
requirements to ensure a day in court for powerful
interest groups while shutting the door on people with
causes for which it has little sympathy.

The requirement that a party have "standing," for
example, means that a person may not challenge a law
in court unless he has a real stake in the outcome of the
lawsuit. The Court did not hesitate to relax this standing requirement in 1978, when it wanted to reach out
to support the nuclear power industry by upholding a
law that put a ceiling on the dollar amount for which
people could sue a utility company if one of its reactors
blew up or melted down. But the door was slammed

shut every bit as fast in 1982, when a group of taxpayers tried to sue the government for giving federal land to a religious institution, and in 1984 when a group of black parents tried to sue the Internal Revenue Service for failing to fulfill its legal duty to cut off special tax benefits to private schools that practiced racial discrimination. In its 1983 decision in *Los Angeles v. Lyons*, the Burger Court went so far as to tell a man, who was nearly choked to death by police when he was stopped for a minor traffic violation, that he had no standing to sue in order to change the police stranglehold policy because he had been strangled only once and could not prove that he would be strangled again. Lawsuits against entire police departments to gain relief from widespread and demonstrably recurring police brutality have met with the same fate. It is not hard to imagine how Senate confirmation of additional Justices fond of and adept at this sort of judicial shell game would make the situation even worse.

IGNORING THE OUTSIDER'S PERSPECTIVE

When presented with claims that an official act discriminates against a particular group, the Burger Court has tended to look at the problem from the perspective of the party benefiting from the discrimination. Those who always look at charges of unequal treatment from the viewpoint of the people who are on top rather than through the eyes of those at the bottom, or from the perspective of the insiders rather than from the position of those who are left out, predictably tend to miss the point.

Thus, when students contended that the denial of government financial aid for education to those who failed to register for the draft hurt less wealthy students more than the rich, their argument fell on deaf ears. The 1984 Supreme Court dismissed this discrimination argument with the terse observation that the law treated all nonregistrants equally—by denying financial aid to rich and poor alike!

In addressing charges of discrimination brought against employee health insurance plans that pay for such things as circumcision and vasectomies but do not cover pregnancy, the Burger Court held that there was no discrimination because pregnancy is an "extra," an additional risk unique to women. This is so, of course, only if one looks at it from the male point of view. From the woman's perspective, it is circumcision that looks like an "extra."

Or consider the case of the citizens who sued their city when it officially sponsored a Christmas nativity scene. The Court weighed the benefit of promoting the holiday spirit against what it saw as the remote cost of an incidental endorsement of one religion over others. It dismissed as trivial the question of whether official endorsement of a Christian symbol sends a message to nonadherents that they are outsiders, not full members of the community. The Court's position, in essence, was that the city's official crèche was no big deal; if any non-Christians were alienated by it, that was *their* problem. Who could fail to hear in this statement an echo of the nineteenth-century Court that once told blacks that if they felt insulted and degraded by being forced to sit in the back of the train and use separate public rest rooms, it was their imagination. If we interpret a message from the position of those who send it, we rarely perceive the offense it gives to those who are told that they are outsiders.

Still, the Burger Court's fifteen years from 1970 to 1985 have not produced the judicial counterrevolution that many expected from that Court. To a significant degree, the reason is that most of the Justices of the Supreme Court through the 1970s and early 1980s have had some respect for precedent and a commitment to the rule of law. The Court has thus maintained a certain equilibrium. As a result, many of the controversial innovations of the Warren Court became relatively secure landmarks that have guided the Burger Court as it has continued to chart the Constitution's course. The Supreme Court as it stood in 1984 usually preferred to tinker with doctrines rather than to rethink them, curbing government encroachment here, trimming back the costly consequences of egalitarianism there. What is left in place by this practice of continuous adjustment is a core of enduring principles. But we must remember that although those principles have survived so far, they are not of themselves immortal. If we want them to thrive, we must choose with great care the nine people who guard them.

Chapter Eight

THE ADVICE AND CONSENT OF THE SENATE

So far we have explored the history of Supreme Court appointments, and have described a model for the Senate to follow in carrying out its constitutional duty to provide advice and consent. To some extent that model *assumes* an active role for both the Senate and the President without asking what would happen if the political branches became too aggressive in the assertion of their prerogatives. Nor have we yet considered the characteristics of the Senate that make it uniquely qualified to play a major role in appointing Justices of the Supreme Court.

On so weighty a matter as the appointment of life-tenured Justices to the third branch of government, one might expect the Constitution to be full of ready answers to our questions about the roles of the President and the Senate. But, as we have seen, those who seek answers by "strictly construing" the document's language—if they are honest with themselves—are bound to be disappointed. Our great charter deals with the appointment process, the subject of this entire book, in a few short phrases in its second Article: the President "shall nominate, and by and with the Advice and Consent of the Senate, shall appoint . . . Judges of the Supreme Court. . . ." We now know that it would be a mistake to read this language and conclude that the President, like a caesar of old, is expected to bring his nominee into the coliseum for a simple "thumbs up" or "thumbs down" from the assembled Senators. But the Constitution also leaves more vexing problems unresolved. What if the Senators continuously refused to confirm the President's choices until he nominated a candidate of *their* choosing? Or what if the Congress reduced the size of the Supreme Court by legislation, so that the President had no vacancy to fill? What if the President refused to compromise with the Senate, and consistently nominated candidates whom the Senate deemed unworthy of its "consent"? And how should the nation reconcile itself to the spectacle of its two political branches locked in an eyeball-to-eyeball grudge match, each waiting for the other to blink, while the Supreme Court shrinks as Justices die or retire?

These are *not* hypothetical questions out of a professor's imagination. Some version of each of these scenarios has occurred in our history. Each time such a crisis arises, it tests the boundaries of our ideas about who should choose Supreme Court Justices. Both the President and the Senate have, on occasion, overplayed the parts that the Constitution assigns them in the appointment drama; and the Justices of the Supreme Court have sometimes crept onto the stage to usurp a role for which they were never cast.

THE APPOINTMENT WALTZ: DISCORD ON THE DANCE FLOOR

For most of the past two hundred years the Senate and the President have been cooperative, if not always congenial, partners in the dance of Supreme Court appointments choreographed by the Constitution's terse instructions. Although the two have often disagreed on the choice of music, and have occasionally stepped on each other's toes, the affair has, by and large, been a successful one. But occasionally the harmony has been shattered by a knock-down-drag-out public brawl.

A beleaguered President Andrew Johnson tried in 1866 to fill the vacant seat on the Supreme Court created a year earlier by the death of Justice John Catron. But the Radical Republican Senate, which would later conduct a trial of Johnson after his impeachment by the House, would have none of it. Instead of acting on Johnson's nomination of Attorney General Henry Stanbery, the Congress passed a bill reducing the size of the Court, so that Johnson had no seat to fill. When Justice James Wayne died in July of 1867, his seat was also eliminated. The Court was down to eight Justices. This is where things stood when Ulysses S. Grant was inaugurated in March of 1869.

Within a month of Grant's assumption of the Presidency, Congress resumed its game of musical chairs and restored one of the missing seats to the Supreme Court. Grant, a Republican war hero facing a Senate that held five times as many Republicans as Democrats, expected little difficulty with his nomination of Attorney General Ebenezer Hoar to the Court. Yet the nomination immediately ran into trouble with Senate radicals who deemed Hoar too moderate for having opposed President Johnson's impeachment and having supported an expanded civil service system as an alternative to government patronage. Even before the Hoar nomination was formally announced, it was vigorously opposed in many quarters.

December 15, 1869, saw two critical developments in the controversy. Grant decided to stand his ground and formally nominated Hoar for the new seat. But at the same time, Justice Robert Grier announced his resignation, to take effect the following February. Grier suggested that he be replaced by Joseph P. Bradley, while President Grant was said to prefer William Strong (both men would eventually become Justices).

With the stakes thus raised by a second appointment, a Senate already angered by Johnson's and Grant's previous nominations decided that it had had enough of letting Presidents do the choosing. Within hours of Grier's announcement, some Senators began to circulate a petition urging the appointment of former Secretary of War Edwin Stanton to the Supreme Court. By the end of the week the petition had been signed by a majority of both houses of Congress and delivered to President Grant. The Senate had construed very broadly indeed its power to give "advice," and its advice to the

President came in the form of a list of acceptable nominations exactly one name long.

President Grant initially resisted; Stanton had been a political rival and was also considered by many to be an "arrogant opportunist" with a "temperament such as to make him a doubtful acquisition to the Bench." But the Senate would not budge, and in the meantime Grant's nomination of Hoar was in limbo. It seemed possible to trade Senate confirmation of Hoar for the President's nomination of Stanton, so the President relented. On December 19, 1869, he sent Stanton's name to the Senate, where it was confirmed within hours by an overwhelming margin, even though Justice Grier's retirement was still two months away. President Grant's reluctant acceptance of the Senate's "nominee" was all for naught; Edwin Stanton had a heart attack and died four days after his confirmation. Aparently a dead Justice of its choosing was not the Senate's idea of a victory, because a few weeks later the Senate refused to confirm Hoar by a vote of 33 to 24. Almost five years had passed since Justice Catron died and created a vacancy on the Supreme Court, but the Senate was in no hurry to fill it. Grant's next nominee, Joseph P. Bradley—Justice Grier's own choice for his replacement—was eventually appointed to the Court in 1870.

The Hoar/Stanton debacle was not the first time that the Supreme Court—and the nation—waited while the President and the Senate locked horns. From December 1843 to August 1846 the Supreme Court lacked its full complement of nine Justices; the Court's bench was down to seven members twice during that three-year period. The Senate spent those years wrestling with the choices of President Tyler, who got only one confirmation out of six nominations, and President Polk, who needed two nominations to fill Justice Baldwin's seat. The remaining Justices proceeded with the Court's business as best they could, with the inevitable consequence that a minority of the full Supreme Court bench often decided constitutional controversies for an entire nation.

A THIRD PARTNER IN THE WALTZ:
THE SUPREME COURT CUTS IN

Whatever questions the Constitution leaves unanswered about the appointment process, it is clear that it envisions a joint effort by the President and the Senate. The Supreme Court is to be shaped by the two political branches; the unelected Justices do not constitute a self-selecting constitutional priesthood. Yet a tendency of the Justices to try to handpick their own colleagues and successors emerged early in the Court's history. Early-nineteenth-century Justices often recommended candidates for nomination. In 1850, Justices Benjamin Curtis and John Catron went so far as to collect flattering letters from every member of the Court when they persuaded President Franklin Pierce to nominate John Campbell to an open seat. Later in the century an even more disturbing practice began to emerge—Justices suggesting candidates to fill the seats they were leaving behind, such as Justice Robert Grier's pick of Joseph Bradley as his "successor" and Justice Samuel Miller's "designation" of Henry Brown as the man who should replace him upon his death.

The prospect of an almost hereditary Supreme Court came closest to becoming a reality in the early years of this century, under the hand of William Howard Taft, who served both as Chief Executive and as Chief Justice. Recall that as President, Taft appointed six Justices in the years 1909 to 1912. As Chief Justice from 1921 to 1930, Taft in turn engineered the appointment of at least three more Justices of his choosing. The judicial predilections of one man thus dominated the Supreme Court from 1910 to 1937; for fourteen of those years, a majority of the Court—sometimes even six Justices— were Taft selections.

Although President Taft had previously announced his commitment to putting vigorous, younger men on the Court, one of his first nominations was the startling and puzzling choice of the sixty-six-year-old Justice Edward White to become Chief Justice in 1910; Taft passed over a younger candidate widely considered much more qualified, Justice Charles Evans Hughes. Taft explained the method in his madness some years later, when he told President Warren Harding that Chief Justice White "had said he was holding the office for me and that he would give it back to me in a Republican administration." White served as Chief Justice for eleven years, and even turned down his pension to remain on the bench. Shortly after Republican Harding took over the presidency from Democrat Woodrow Wilson, the half-deaf and nearly blind Chief Justice White—true to his word—died. Through his careful appointments as President and his subsequent manipulation of President Harding, Taft effectively appointed himself Chief Justice, joining two other Justices he had chosen when he occupied the Oval Office.

Shortly after his automatic confirmation as Chief Justice—he was confirmed by the Senate on the same day that he was nominated by President Harding—Taft successfully lobbied for the appointment of George Sutherland as the next addition to the Court. And in 1922 he conducted a fierce campaign to secure the nomination of Minnesota conservative Pierce Butler. Taft organized a letter-writing campaign, rallied the Catholic Church hierarchy behind Butler, and smeared the alternative choices—dismissing the eminent Judge Benjamin Cardozo as a "Jew and a Democrat," and the distinguished Judge Learned Hand as "almost certainly a dissenter." This unjudicial conduct paid off handsomely—President Harding nominated Butler and later added Edward Sanford, Taft's close personal friend, to the Court. Taft's domination of Supreme Court appointments through the offices of both President and Chief Justice led to a consistently conservative, anti-labor, anti-New Deal Court of his own design. This was the entrenched constitutional philosophy that haunted the infamous *Lochner* era and brought the Supreme Court as an institution to the brink of disaster in the Court-packing controversy of 1937. This story illustrates, as no hypothetical tale could, the perils of allowing the brethren to make of the Supreme Court a self-perpetuating aristocracy.

WALTZING WITH AN ASSERTIVE PARTNER

When both partners in the appointment waltz insist on leading, or when they move to the beat of different drummers, the appointment process sometimes breaks down. When that has happened, the President and Senate have been distracted from their other work, and the Supreme Court has had to face its task of constitutional decision-making with diminished resources. So we might fairly ask why anyone would advocate such an active role for the Senate in choosing Supreme Court Justices. Virtually automatic Senate acquiescence in presidential nominations might do damage to the equilibrium of the Court and to the course of constitutional justice, but such a policy would at least spare the nation the spectacle of the two political branches contorted in a relentless struggle over appointments, or trapped in a potentially endless stalemate. In such contests it is the Supreme Court and the nation who are the real losers, not the Senate or the President.

But the prospect of occasionally protracted confrontations does not provide a sufficient rationale for the Senate to abdicate its duties of meaningful advice and consent. Presidents and Senators, like the rest of us, recognize the ultimate futility of stalemates and the danger they pose to the integrity both of the political branches and of the Supreme Court. History records that—in the vast majority of cases—respect for the other branch, the need to get on with the practical business of running a great nation, and the Constitution's own system of checks and balances have been sufficient to keep the appointment process on track. The executive and legislative branches, while not always thrilled with the prospect, manage to live with each other because they have to: the President must respect the Senate's power to veto his nominations, and the Senate must respect the President's power to select potential Supreme Court Justices.

WALTZING ON A CROWDED DANCE FLOOR

Why should Senators undertake an assertive role in the appointment of Supreme Court Justices? Don't the Senators already have more than enough to do? Many would agree that the Senate's self-conscious image as the "world's greatest deliberative body" is rather tarnished these days. In recent elections, several state governors have refused to become their parties' candidates for the Senate because they have no desire to subject themselves to the "the 535-ring circus" that is the modern Congress. In recent decades the Senate has become significantly more fragmented. The pressures of legions of lobbyists and the demands of continuous political campaigning lead too many in Congress to avoid facing critical national problems by immersing themselves in the administrative details of their own bureaucracies; they become "prisoners of trivia."

The impact on the legislative product of the crushing work load and the torrent of bills and amendments is alarming—and sometimes amusing. In 1981 the telephone number of a woman named Rita was enacted into law because it had been scribbled in the margin of the only copy of an amendment being voted on, and the following day it was duly transcribed into the printed copy of the bill. The all-night legislative binges with which Congress closes its sessions have become an annual tradition. As they struggle to keep the federal government financially afloat and to clean up unfinished business, bleary-eyed Senators and Representatives cast their votes with little attention to whether they are voting to limit imports of Japanese cars, to create an enormous new tax loophole, or to amend Rita's phone number. Why, with the floor so crowded, should we ask the Senate to make room on its dance card for the appointment waltz?

The responsibility of closely reviewing Supreme Court nominations does not tax the Senate in the same way as its legislative duties do. In confirming or rejecting the President's nominees, there is no need for the Senate to muster within its ranks a spirit of compromise, nor to piece together a carefully crafted legislative consensus. The appointment process requires the Senate only to react, not to create. And since what matters most is that one hundred Senators, of diverse backgrounds and philosophies, individually take a good, hard look at both the nominee and at the Supreme Court the nominee will join, the Senate's role can be fulfilled even if each Senator goes in a different direction. A concerted, collective effort by the upper house of Congress to articulate a vision of the Constitution's future, and to scrutinize potential Justices in that vision's light, is of course the ideal. But the nation will also be well served by the attentions of individual Senators who bring their varied experiences and insights to bear on the question of confirmation, and who vote their separate consciences.

THE VIRTUES OF THE SENATE AS AN EQUAL PARTNER

A brief look at how the Senate came to have a role in the appointment process is illuminating. One of the original drafts of the Constitution envisioned the Congress itself actually electing the Justices. And the Constitutional Convention adopted a draft that had the Senate alone choose the members of the Supreme Court. This scheme in fact remained in the draft until the final days of the Convention, after the idea of appointment by presidential nomination with Senate consent was twice voted down. Finally, the current provision was accepted—as a compromise between those who desired a stronger President and those who envisioned a weaker one.

But as the times have changed, so have the institutions of Presidency and Senate that are involved in the process of appointing Justices. The "original intent" of the Framers of our Constitution should not be, and indeed cannot be, the final authority in constitutional discourse on this issue any more than on others. The reasons for dividing the appointment power between the Senate and the President two hundred years ago are not necessarily identical with the reasons for such a division of power today.

The Framers thought they were creating a Presidency that would be won by a man—women couldn't even *vote* then—elected by a small, elite body, the Electoral College, and a Senate selected by the legislatures of the states. Today the President is elected in a monumental festival of microphones, TV cameras, popular campaigning, and ideological mass movements—hardly the insular body of civic leaders on whom the Framers relied to put the nation's highest office in safe hands. And ever since the ratification of the Seventeenth Amendment in 1913, Senators have been directly elected by the people rather than selected by the state legislatures; many Senate races in the last decade have taken on the aura and trappings of mini (and sometimes *not* so mini)—presidential races. For these reasons, whatever notions the authors of the Constitution held about authority and legitimacy must be reconsidered in light of the significant changes in the way we pick our President and our Senators. The electoral process for both is far more democratic now. And with respect to Supreme Court appointments, this is the common denominator of the Senate's virtues as compared with the President's: the Senate is more diverse, more representative, more accountable.

Unlike the President, who can never be more than one person at a time, the Senate as a body has a hundred different heads. The Senate comprises members from all fifty states, and will usually include members of both genders, many different religious and ethnic backgrounds, and, sometimes, members of different races. Senators are of different ages and come from different occupations and different backgrounds. Although hardly a mirror of our nation's broad cultural and racial diversity, the Senate will always be more varied in geographic and socioeconomic characteristics than a single person in the White House could ever be. These virtues of diversity were recognized even in *The Federalist Papers*, where the Senate's role was seen in part as ensuring that the President did not simply pick nominees "coming from the same State to which he belonged."

The need for diversity among the voices that question and confirm Supreme Court Justices is greater today than ever before. Although the nation has grown more homogeneous under the influence of convenient travel and the mass media, critical differences remain. And while at one time some diversity on the Court was maintained through customs like having a "New York seat" or a "Jewish seat," many of these traditions are no longer observed and would in any event be insufficient to create the kind of balanced Supreme Court we desire. The hopes expressed by some that the pioneering service of Justice Thurgood Marshall (the first black Justice) and Justice Sandra Day O'Connor (the first woman on the Court) would result in the establishment of a "minority seat" or a "woman's seat" must be tempered by the recognition that such fragile entitlements can pass away. We cannot rely on the willingness of Presidents to maintain, much less expand, such traditions. Only the active involvement of the Senate, pressing the hopes and dreams of people from all regions, all walks of life, can keep the Court from becoming narrow, isolated, and removed from the many and varied threads that make up the rich tapestry we call America.

The Senate represents diversity in our country in another, possibly more important way. Although the President is both Chief Executive and the leader of his party, the Senate inevitably includes members of both parties, and therefore reflects a more diverse range of political philosophies. It takes only a cursory glance to appreciate the fallacy in suggesting that since the President is elected by a majority of voters, it would be democratic to let him alone choose the Justices. After all, even the fortunate winner of a 60 per cent majority has failed to gain the support of the other 40 per cent of the country. True, our winner-take-all system does not give the substantial minority anything resembling control of the presidency for 40 per cent of the time. Yet there seems no sound reason why the person chosen by just 60 per cent of the voters—what we call a landslide—

should be allowed 100 per cent of the time to select Supreme Court Justices, and perhaps a full Court majority, reflecting his views alone.

This is of particular concern in a case where a President with a less stunning victory—such as Abraham Lincoln, who won with but 39 per cent of the popular vote in a four-way election, or Benjamin Harrison, who took office with *fewer* popular votes than his opponent, Grover Cleveland, and won only in the Electoral College—may be in a position to name four or more Justices. But the point remains strong even when the President wins by a landslide, because the size of the avalanche is irrelevant to the question whether the President has a mandate to remake the Supreme Court in his own image. In this century, only the election of F.D.R. in 1936 could honestly be said to have given the President such a mandate, because that was the one campaign in which Supreme Court appointments surfaced as a major issue and in which the victor won by a mandate-sized margin. When the President is elected on such a constitutionally extraneous platform as prosperity, patriotism, and personality, the electorate has not given the President a blank check to redirect the Supreme Court, because the campaign did not draw on that particular account. And, finally, there is the puzzle of the nine Justices nominated by men not elected to the presidency at all—those who have succeeded to that office from the vice presidency.

The character of the Senate, which always includes a minority party, lends itself to representing the full range of relevant views in the appointment process—and properly so. For the people have spoken in electing the Senate as well as the President. And, in their own way, the Senators represent the popular will as much as, or more than, the President does. Indeed, if the "people" have installed a majority of one party in the Senate, and the leader of a different party in the White House, it becomes flatly false to assert that *either* party was chosen to choose our Justices. This is not to say that Justices should be apportioned to political parties in the way that a parliamentary system dispenses coalition seats in a European cabinet. But this *is* to say that seats on the Court should not be viewed as slots in an American cabinet—as policy-making roles rightfully given only to the President's lieutenants because that is "what the people wanted." Unity *within* the executive branch may be essential; unity *between* the two political branches, especially when the issue is the shape and direction of the judiciary, is not.

The Senate represents a more lasting view of the American majority as well. Unlike the President, chosen by one potentially ephemeral snapshot of the electorate on one Tuesday in one November, the Senate is really *three* pictures of public sentiment, superimposed to create a multidimensional image of a varied people. Since Senators rotate their terms, with one-third of the hundred being elected in each even-numbered year, and with each serving a six-year term, the Senate reflects the majority of the voters through a longer, moving picture. And, like any moving picture, the Senate may be better able to capture a fuller and truer image of the country than any single snapshot could. Thus, in 1930, with public discontent over economic conservatism on the rise, the progressive and responsive Senate wisely resisted Herbert Hoover's nomination of Judge John Parker and instead confirmed Justice Owen Roberts to the Court, bringing to that tribunal the Justice who "switched" in time to lead the Court to uphold vital New Deal legislation.

Active Senate involvement also tends to ensure that Supreme Court majorities are not allowed to perpetuate themselves by selecting their successors. Although the Constitution, nearing its bicentennial, is to be passed down from generation to generation, its reading and interpretation must to some degree change to reflect the new realities of each new era, and must change by means more continuous and evolutionary than frequent resort to the always difficult amendment process would permit. The Court cannot be the organic institution that it must be in our evolving society if one constitutional philosophy—adopted by one set of Justices—is foisted upon successive generations as the Court becomes a virtually hereditary body.

As we saw with Grant's capitulation to the choice of Justice Grier, and more dramatically in the three decades of Taft's dominance of the selection process, a President is far more likely than the Senate to be susceptible to a Justice's suggestions for the Court. The Senate, if only because its members are more numerous and respond to a far wider range of influences, is much less likely to be herded into selecting a Justice's choice for the Court or the Court's choice for itself. Justices aware of a Senate's active role are also less likely to attempt to exert their influence, for almost any effort to affect the opinions of a body like the Senate is sure to become public in short order. Although fear of public exposure and backlash seems never to have bothered Chief Justice Taft, sensibilities in this media age are more attuned to ethical taints. Senate participation in the selection process thus preserves the dynamic element of constitutional choice by ensuring that a changing majority, and not any fixed one, picks the Justices.

The Twenty-second Amendment's limit on presidential tenure adds yet another element to the equation. Unlike any Senator, a President entering his second term knows as a matter of constitutional mandate that it must be his last. As a "lame duck," such a President faces a situation unique in American politics—a political career that has reached the highest plateau, and now is fixed to end on a given date. The lame-duck President comes to his second term with extensive political debts owed to those who supported his two electoral successes, but with no real stake in a political future. Thus he is free to mortgage our constitutional future to discharge, perhaps in the best of faith, the political debts he has accumulated over the years both to individuals and to constituencies. The Senate, on the other hand, is always filled with members pondering their political tomorrows. They are therefore more accountable. This is what the Senate has recognized when, on six different occasions, it has refused to confirm a Supreme

Court momination made by a lame-duck President after he has lost reelection or has chosen not to run again.

There is one situation in which the Senate must be particularly wary in reviewing appointments—whenever the President nominates a Senator to the Supreme Court. Here the Senate's institutional prerogatives do not so vigorously counteract those of the President. By tradition, the Senate confirms such nominations with almost no investigation and with amazing, rather than deliberate, speed. Even such mediocre selections as President Harry Truman's nominations of his former fellow Senators Harold Burton and Sherman Minton can be slipped through the Senate with the lubrication of "senatorial comity." The case of F.D.R.'s 1937 nomination of Alabama Senator Hugo Black bears reflection as well. Although Black was seen as a controversial radical by many in the Senate, he was confirmed in five short days—he was, after all, a member of The Club One Hundred. Three weeks later, a series of Pulitzer Prize–winning articles revealed that Justice Black had been a dues-paying member of the Ku Klux Klan, and had been given one of its highest awards. A debate gripped the nation, with many major newspapers calling for the new Justice's resignation. But by the time the information came out, the former Senator had been confirmed and sworn in and was on vacation in Europe. Although Hugo Black probably would and should have been confirmed in any event, the country should at least have had the timely knowledge that it lacked about his past—knowledge it was denied by the Senate's hasty action on the nomination of "one of its own."

Nonetheless, the Senate will, and should, remain the ultimate guardian of Supreme Court nominations. The vigil must be well kept, for with the nomination power a President's influence over the country can extend for years, sometimes decades, beyond any popular or political limit. When we select Supreme Court Justices, we create a judicial time capsule: we freeze an image of the Constitution that one person holds today and send it off to be observed by, and to shape, the future. No other national office in American government operates in this time-delay manner. A President's decisions about war and peace, or about the economy, may stay with us for years to come, but at least the Presidents themselves are gone in, at most, eight years. A Supreme Court Justice may serve four times as long. This is not to suggest that Justices should have terms that end when the President's does. This *is* to suggest that we need to heed more voices, and to think more deeply, when such grave decisions are made, projecting power that will affect us—and will shape the ways we live and even the ways we die—for decades to come.

Any suggestion that Supreme Court nominations are the President's to dispense, like the Queen of England's New Year's Day list of knighthoods and titles, ignores how much is at stake when those nominations are made. The next Justice appointed will in all probability still be sitting on the Supreme Court in the year 2001. What constitutional vision will he or she impose on America in the twenty-first century? What votes will that next Justice cast in the coming decades on matters vital to our future? In which historic 5–4 majorities will that Justice's views prove decisive? Which other votes will that Justice's views sway? What landmark opinions, what great dissents, will that Justice write in the continuing dialogue between the Court and the country over the meaning of our Constitution? The answers to these questions *matter*. For the Senate must serve as a fierce and tenacious guardian over access to these nine important chairs. Only a broadly based, aggressively contested, scrupulously considered choice now can ensure that the Supreme Court's constitutional vision will be a bright one.

ALL PERSONS HAVING BUSINESS BEFORE THE SUPREME COURT

The building that houses the Supreme Court has been called a marble palace; it is indeed an imposing structure, loosely modeled on the Parthenon. But while the building occupies a full square block facing the Capitol, the courtroom itself is so small that those who see it for the first time are often shocked that so august a tribunal should conduct its formal proceedings in so compact a chamber. Both the size of the courtroom, and the muffled stillness of its heavily curtained walls, conspire to create an impression of almost ironic intimacy.

Thus, when the Marshal's cry of "Oyez!" is followed by his admonition for "all persons having business before the honorable, the Supreme Court of the United States" to "draw near and give attention," public visitors to the courtroom must be forgiven for supposing that he is surely not addressing *them*. Those with "business" before *this* Honorable Court must be the dark-suited lawyers sitting respectfully at their mahogany tables, the attorneys nervously awaiting their turns to make the oral presentations—typically punctuated by sharp inquiries from the nine figures seated behind the bench—that the Court calls "argument." The parties for whom these lawyers speak, a public visitor is likely to suppose, must in turn include only high public officials—Governors, the President, Senators—and perhaps the colorful private characters whose litigious lives put them on the evening news.

167

Consider the business manager in her late thirties, visiting the nation's capital for the first time and making her brief pilgrimage to the Supreme Court. She is unlikely to think, when she hears the Marshal's admonition, that the reason she could go jogging along the Potomac earlier the same day without worrying that she might be stopped by local police and asked for verifiable proof of her identity and residence is that the very Court whose proceedings she is about to witness held in 1983 that governments in America enjoy no such power of inquiry under our Constitution.

Or consider the woman standing behind her in the public line, a computer programmer in her mid-twenties who lives in Connecticut and is visiting her grandfather in the suburbs of Washington, D.C. She decided that she would catch a glimpse of the Court about which she had read from time to time. Who can blame her for not pausing to recall that she, too, has "business" before this Court—one of whose decisions, in 1965, told her home state that it could not jail her or anyone else for using a contraceptive or search her bedroom for telltale signs that she had used one.

And her grandfather, who did not join her in her visit to the Court, certainly cannot be blamed for his failure to notice that even he may have "business" here: he collects a Social Security check each month only because the Supreme Court in 1937 upheld Congress's power to pass the Social Security Act. And it is this same Court that will lay down the ground rules for deciding whether his granddaughter, or a hospital functionary, or a municipal court judge will control the artificial respirator whose rhythm may one day measure his final hours on earth.

We *all* have business, serious business indeed, before this Honorable Court. What it does—which cases it decides to hear from among the thousands presented to it annually, how it rules in the handful of cases (rarely more than 180) it chooses to take up each year— will powerfully shape, and will often chart, the course of our lives as individuals, as communities, and as a nation. In every aspect of our lives—from the character of the economy and its regulation, to the nature of social life and sexual intimacy, to the very ways we are born and pass our days and die—not even the most passive, restrained, low-profile Supreme Court imaginable can any longer avoid playing a decisive role.

In fact, even the term "role" is misleading: it suggests that the Supreme Court is but one more actor on the legal and political stage—an actor who could, if the casting were just right, be reduced to a bit part. But if we have learned one thing from the history of the Court in the life of our country, it is that the Justices are *not* just so many actors on the stage. To them has fallen a large share of a far more basic function—that of playwright and director. It is the Justices who decide *which roles will be played by whom*: which decisions about hours and wages will be made by government regulators and which will be left to the play of private bargains; which things of value—housing, medical care, legal services, voting opportunities—will be sold only on private markets and which will be available to all as a matter of right; which decisions about birth and death will be made by lawmakers, which will be reserved to medical professionals, and which will be left to the men and women most intimately involved.

However decisions like these are to be made, no conscientious student of the Constitution and its framing can pretend that more than a few of them have already been made for us by those who wrote and ratified the Constitution of the United States. So much of that extraordinary document is written in open-ended and merely suggestive terms that only the barest outline of the production has truly been fixed in advance. A stage direction here, a cue there, a few clear rules about such matters as intermissions and changes of cast—only these are set in constitutional concrete.

For the rest, we have entrusted our fates—our lives, our fortunes, our sacred honor—to a process in which many of the most crucial choices, the choices on which much else depends, must be made by a group of nine inevitably fallible individuals, wearing robes that cannot transform mere mortals into great prophets. We have seen that it is an illusion to suppose that who these nine people actually *are* makes no great difference—that it is a myth that their outlooks and points of view when they come to the Court can be safely ignored because "the law," as a vast and impersonal force, tightly reins them in.

And we have seen that it is equally illusory to suppose that the choices a Justice is likely to make after years on the Supreme Court need not concern us when the initial selection is made because the very process of serving on the Court may make each Justice's votes and views very different from anything we could have predicted when the Justice was named. In fact, as we have seen, it is simply a myth that Presidents, and the rest of us, are likely to be all that surprised. From George Washington's time to Richard Nixon's, what we saw in nominees (or could have seen had we looked closely) was pretty much what we got: there are few real surprises in a Justice's overall trajectory. It's true, of course, that those who begin with open minds tend to grow and change more than those selected for their dogmatic rigidity. But then that, too, should come as no surprise. Pick a Justice with a mind known to be closed or narrow, and we're unlikely to come up with a visionary—a judge who develops the capacity to reconcile freedom with authority, change with continuity, experimentation with tradition.

Picking judges is too important a task to be left to any President: unless the Senate, acting as a continuing body accountable to the nation as a whole, plays an active and thoughtful part—something we have seen it do through much of our history—the way we and our children live and die will be shaped more powerfully by a single official's vision than any electoral mandate on any Tuesday in November could possibly justify.

Especially in periods when a Chief Executive is likely, given the ages of the sitting Justices, to be making *several* appointments to our highest court, each name the President sends to the Senate deserves and demands the closest scrutiny—not only to assess *whether* the nominee is, in some minimal sense, "fit" to serve, but also to evaluate *where* the nominee's service would be likely to lead the Court. For the Court, and with it the country and the Constitution, are cast upon a long and perilous voyage by any such series of appointments. To permit the direction and destination of that voyage to be prefigured by any President's personal philosophy, or personal friendships, without the most searching consideration by a larger and more varied body, is to entrust too much of our destiny to the values and priorities, the wisdom and the restraint, of one individual and a handful of his political advisers.

We owe it to ourselves, and to those we leave behind, to do more than ask God to *save* this Honorable Court while leaving it to the President to *shape* the Court into the distant future. If we confront how deeply each choice of a new Justice can change our lives, then we will, all of us, find ways to educate ourselves, and then to make ourselves heard, each time that fateful choice is made.

SUPREME COURT NOMINATIONS, 1789–1984

NAME	STATE	NAMED BY	AGE WHEN NOMINATED	ACTION
JOHN JAY	N.Y.	Washington	43	Conf.
John Rutledge	S.C.	Washington	50	Conf.
William Cushing	Mass.	Washington	57	Conf.
[Robert H. Harrison]	Md.	Washington	44	Dec.
James Wilson	Pa.	Washington	47	Conf.
John Blair	Va.	Washington	57	Conf.
James Iredell	N.C.	Washington	38	Conf.
Thomas Johnson	Md.	Washington	58	Conf.
William Paterson	N.J.	Washington	47	W/draw
William Paterson*		Washington		Conf.
JOHN RUTLEDGE°		Washington		Rej.
WILLIAM CUSHING°		Washington		Dec.
Samuel Chase	Md.	Washington	54	Conf.
OLIVER ELLSWORTH	Conn.	Washington	50	Conf.
Bushrod Washington	Va.	Adams	36	Conf.
Alfred Moore	N.C.	Adams	44	Conf.
[JOHN JAY°]		Adams		Dec.
JOHN MARSHALL	Va.	Adams	45	Conf.
William Johnson	S.C.	Jefferson	32	Conf.
Henry B. Livingston	N.Y.	Jefferson	49	Conf.
Thomas Todd	Ky.	Jefferson	42	Conf.
[Levi Lincoln]	Mass.	Madison	61	Dec.
[Alexander Wolcott]	Conn.	Madison	52	Rej.
[John Quincy Adams]	Mass.	Madison	43	Dec.
Joseph Story	Mass.	Madison	32	Conf.
Gabriel Duvall	Md.	Madison	58	Conf.
Smith Thompson	N.Y.	Monroe	55	Conf.
Robert Trimble	Ky.	J.Q. Adams	49	Conf.
[John J. Critenden]	Ky.	J.Q. Adams	41	Post.
John McLean	Ohio	Jackson	43	Conf.
Henry Baldwin	Pa.	Jackson	49	Conf.
James M. Wayne	Ga.	Jackson	45	Conf.
[Roger B. Taney]	Md.	Jackson	57	Post.
ROGER B. TANEY*		Jackson		Conf.

VOTE	DATE OF ACTION	DATE RESIGNED	DIED	YEARS ON COURT
	9/26/1789	6/29/1795	5/17/1829	6
	9/26/1789	3/05/1791	6/21/1800	1
	9/26/1789		9/13/1810	21
	9/26/1789		4/20/1790	
	9/26/1789		8/21/1798	9
	9/26/1789	1/27/1796	8/31/1800	6
	2/10/1790		10/20/1799	9
	11/07/1791	3/04/1793	10/26/1819	1
	2/28/1793			
	3/04/1793		9/09/1806	13
(10-14)	12/15/1795			
	1/27/1796			
	1/27/1796		6/19/1811	15
(21-1)	3/04/1796	9/30/1800	11/26/1807	4
	12/20/1798		11/26/1829	31
	12/10/1799	1/26/1804	10/15/1810	4
	12/19/1800			
	1/27/1801		7/06/1835	34
	3/24/1804		8/04/1834	30
	12/17/1806		3/18/1823	16
	3/03/1807		2/07/1826	19
	1/03/1811		4/14/1820	
(9-24)	2/13/1811		6/26/1828	
	2/22/1811		2/23/1848	
	11/18/1811		9/10/1845	
	11/18/1811	1/10/1835	3/06/1844	23
	12/19/1823		12/18/1843	20
(27-5)	5/09/1826		8/25/1828	2
	2/12/1829		7/26/1863	
	3/07/1829		4/04/1861	32
(41-2)	1/06/1830		4/21/1844	14
	1/09/1835		7/05/1867	32
	3/03/1835			
(29-15)	3/15/1836		10/12/1864	28

NAME	STATE	NAMED BY	AGE WHEN NOMINATED	ACTION
Philip P. Barbour	Va.	Jackson	52	Conf.
[William Smith]	Ala.	Jackson	75	Dec.
John Catron	Tenn.	Jackson	51	Conf.
John McKinley	Ala.	Van Buren	57	Conf.
Peter V. Daniel	Va.	Van Buren	56	Conf.
[John C. Spencer]	N.Y.	Tyler	56	Rej.
[Reuben Walworth]	N.Y.	Tyler	55	W/draw
[Edward King]	Pa.	Tyler	50	Post.
[Edward King*]		Tyler		W/draw
Samuel Nelson	N.Y.	Tyler	52	Conf.
[John M. Read]	Pa.	Tyler	47	None
[George Woodward]	Pa.	Polk	36	Rej.
Levi Woodbury	N.H.	Polk	56	Conf.
Robert C. Grier	Pa.	Polk	52	Conf.
Benjamin R. Curtis	Mass.	Fillmore	42	Conf.
[Edward A. Bradford]	La.	Fillmore	38	None
[George E. Badger]	N.C.	Fillmore	57	Post.
[William C. Micou]	La.	Fillmore	47	None
John A. Campbell	Ala.	Pierce	41	Conf.
Nathan Clifford	Maine	Buchanan	54	Conf.
[Jeremiah S. Black]	Pa.	Buchanan	51	Rej.
Noah H. Swayne	Ohio	Lincoln	57	Conf.
Samuel F. Miller	Iowa	Lincoln	46	Conf.
David Davis	Ill.	Liincoln	47	Conf.
Stephen J. Field	Calif.	Lincoln	46	Conf.
SALMON P. CHASE	Ohio	Lincoln	56	Conf.
[Henry Stanbery]	Ohio	Johnson	63	None
[Ebenezer R. Hoar]	Mass.	Grant	53	Rej.
[Edwin M. Stanton]	Pa.	Grant	55	Conf.
William Strong	Pa.	Grant	61	Conf.
Joseph P. Bradley	N.J.	Grant	56	Conf.
Ward Hunt	N.Y.	Grant	62	Conf.
[GEORGE H. WILLIAMS]	Ore.	Grant	50	W/draw

VOTE	DATE OF ACTION	DATE RESIGNED	DIED	YEARS ON COURT
(30-11)	3/15/1836		2/25/1841	5
(23-18)	3/08/1837		6/10/1840	
(28-15)	3/08/1837		5/30/1865	28
	9/25/1837		7/19/1852	15
(22-5)	3/02/1841		5/31/1860	19
(21-26)	1/31/1844		5/18/1855	
	6/17/1844		11/27/1867	
	6/15/1844			
	2/07/1845		5/08/1873	
	2/14/1845	11/28/1872	12/13/1873	27
	no action		11/29/1874	
(20-29)	1/22/1846		5/10/1875	
	1/03/1846		9/04/1851	5
	8/04/1846	1/31/1870	9/26/1870	23
	12/29/1851	9/30/1857	9/15/1874	5
	no action		11/22/1872	
	2/11/1853		5/11/1866	
	no action		4/16/1854	
	3/25/1853	4/26/1861	3/13/1889	8
(26-23)	1/12/1858		7/25/1881	23
(25-26)	2/21/1861		8/19/1883	
(38-1)	1/24/1862	1/24/1881	6/08/1884	19
	7/16/1862		10/13/1890	28
	12/08/1862	3/07/1877	6/26/1886	14
	3/10/1863	12/01/1897	4/09/1899	34
	12/06/1864		5/07/1873	8
	no action		6/26/1881	
(24-33)	2/03/1870		1/31/1895	
(46-11)	12/20/1869		12/24/1869	
	2/18/1870	12/14/1880	8/19/1895	10
(46-9)	3/21/1870		1/22/1892	21
	12/11/1872	1/07/1882	3/24/1886	9
	1/08/1874		4/04/1910	

NAME	STATE	NAMED BY	AGE WHEN NOMINATED	ACTION
[CALEB CUSHING]	Mass.	Grant	73	W/draw
MORRISON R. WAITE	Ohio	Grant	57	Conf.
John M. Harlan	Ky.	Hayes	44	Conf.
William B. Woods	Ga.	Hayes	56	Conf.
[Stanley Matthews]	Ohio	Hayes	56	None
Stanley Matthews*		Garfield		Conf.
Horace Gray	Mass.	Arthur	53	Conf.
[Roscoe Conkling]	N.Y.	Arthur	52	Dec.
Samuel Blatchford	N.Y.	Arthur	62	Conf.
Lucius Q.C. Lamar	Miss.	Cleveland	62	Conf.
MELVILLE W. FULLER	Ill.	Cleveland	55	Conf.
David J. Brewer	Kan.	Harrison	52	Conf.
Henry B. Brown	Mich.	Harrison	54	Conf.
George Shiras Jr.	Pa.	Harrison	60	Conf.
Howell E. Jackson	Tenn.	Harrison	60	Conf.
[William Hornblower]	N.Y.	Cleveland	42	Rej.
[Wheeler H. Peckham]	N.Y.	Cleveland	61	Rej.
Edward D. White	La.	Cleveland	48	Conf.
Rufus W. Peckham	N.Y.	Cleveland	57	Conf.
Joseph McKenna	Calif.	McKinley	54	Conf.
Oliver W. Holmes	Mass.	Roosevelt	61	Conf.
William R. Day	Ohio	Roosevelt	53	Conf.
William H. Moody	Mass.	Roosevelt	52	Conf.
Horace H. Lurton	Tenn.	Taft	65	Conf.
EDWARD D. WHITE°		Taft		Conf.
Charles E. Hughes	N.Y.	Taft	48	Conf.
Willis Van Devanter	Wyo.	Taft	51	Conf.
Joseph R. Lamar	Ga.	Taft	53	Conf.
Mahlon Pitney	N.J.	Taft	54	Conf.
James McReynolds	Tenn.	Wilson	52	Conf.
Louis D. Brandeis	Mass.	Wilson	59	Conf.
John H. Clarke	Ohio	Wilson	58	Conf.

VOTE	DATE OF ACTION	DATE RESIGNED	DIED	YEARS ON COURT
	1/13/1874		1/02/1879	
(63-0)	1/21/1874		3/23/1888	14
	11/29/1877		10/14/1911	34
(39-8)	12/21/1880		5/14/1887	6
	no action			
(24-23)	5/12/1881		3/22/1889	7
(51-5)	12/20/1881	7/09/1902	9/15/1902	20
(39-12)	3/02/1882		4/18/1888	
	3/27/1882		7/07/1893	11
(32-28)	1/16/1888		1/23/1893	5
(41-20)	7/20/1888		7/04/1910	22
(53-11)	12/18/1889		3/28/1910	20
	12/29/1890	5/28/1906	9/04/1913	15
	7/26/1892	2/23/1903	8/02/1924	10
	2/18/1893		8/08/1895	2
(24-30)	1/15/1894		6/16/1914	
(32–41)	2/16/1894		9/27/1905	
	2/19/1894		5/19/1921	17
	12/09/1895		10/24/1909	13
	1/21/1898	1/05/1925	11/21/1926	26
	12/04/1902	1/12/1932	3/06/1935	29
	2/23/1903	11/13/1922	7/09/1923	19
	12/12/1906	11/20/1910	7/02/1917	3
	12/20/1909		7/12/1914	4
	12/12/1910			10°
	5/02/1910	6/10/1916	8/27/1948	6
	12/15/1910	6/02/1937	2/08/1941	26
	12/15/1910		1/02/1916	5
(50-26)	3/13/1912	12/31/1922	12/09/1924	10
(44-6)	8/29/1914	1/31/1941	8/24/1946	26
(47-22)	6/01/1916	2/13/1939	10/05/1941	22
	7/24/1916	7/18/1922	3/22/1945	6

NAME	STATE	NAMED BY	AGE WHEN NOMINATED	ACTION
WILLIAM H. TAFT	Ohio	Harding	63	Conf.
George Sutherland	Utah	Harding	60	Conf.
Pierce Butler	Minn.	Harding	56	Conf.
Edward T. Sanford	Tenn.	Harding	57	Conf.
Harlan F. Stone	N.Y.	Coolidge	52	Conf.
CHARLES E. HUGHES°		Hoover		Conf.
[John J. Parker]	N.C.	Hoover	44	Rej.
Owen J. Roberts	Pa.	Hoover	55	Conf.
Benjamin N. Cardozo	N.Y.	Hoover	61	Conf.
Hugo L. Black	Ala.	Roosevelt	51	Conf.
Stanley F. Reed	Ky.	Roosevelt	53	Conf.
Felix Frankfurter	Mass.	Roosevelt	56	Conf.
William O. Douglas	Conn.	Roosevelt	40	Conf.
Frank Murphy	Mich	Roosevelt	49	Conf.
HARLAN F. STONE°		Roosevelt		Conf.
James F. Byrnes	S.C.	Roosevelt	62	Conf.
Robert H. Jackson	N.Y.	Roosevelt	49	Conf.
Wiley B. Rutledge	Iowa	Roosevelt	48	Conf.
Harold H. Burton	Ohio	Truman	57	Conf.
FRED M. VINSON	Ky.	Truman	56	Conf.
Tom C. Clark	Texas	Truman	49	Conf.
Sherman Minton	Ind.	Truman	58	Conf.
EARL WARREN	Calif.	Eisenhower	62	Conf.
John M. Harlan	N.Y.	Eisenhower	55	Conf.
William J. Brennan	N.J.	Eisenhower	50	Conf.
Charles E. Whittaker	Mo.	Eisenhower	56	Conf.
Potter Stewart	Ohio	Eisenhower	43	Conf.
Byron R. White	Colo.	Kennedy	44	Conf.
Arthur J. Goldberg	Ill.	Kennedy	54	Conf.
Abe Fortas	Tenn.	Johnson	55	Conf.
Thurgood Marshall	N.Y.	Johnson	59	Conf.
[ABES FORTAS°]		Johnson		W/draw
[Homer Thornberry]	Texas	Johnson	59	None

VOTE	DATE OF ACTION	DATE RESIGNED	DIED	YEARS ON COURT
	6/30/1921	2/03/1930	3/08/1930	8
	9/05/1922	1/17/1938	7/18/1942	15
(61-8)	12/21/1922		11/16/1939	17
	1/29/1923		3/08/1930	7
(71-6)	2/05/1925		4/22/1946	16
(52-26)	2/13/1930	7/01/1941	8/27/1948	11°
(39-41)	5/07/1930		3/17/1958	
	5/20/1930	7/31/1945	5/17/1955	15
	2/24/1932		7/09/1938	6
(63-16)	8/17/1937	9/17/1971	9/25/1971	34
	1/25/1938	2/26/1957	4/02/1980	19
	1/17/1939	8/28/1962	2/22/1965	23
(62-4)	4/04/1939	11/12/1975	1/19/1980	36
	1/15/1940		7/19/1949	9
	6/27/1941		4/22/1946	5°
	6/12/1941	10/03/1942	4/09/1972	1
	7/07/1941		10/09/1954	13
	2/08/1943		9/10/1949	6
	9/19/1945	10/13/1958	10/28/1964	13
	6/20/1946		9/08/1953	7
(73-8)	8/18/1949	6/12/1967	6/13/1977	18
(48-16)	10/04/1949	10/15/1956	4/09/1965	7
	3/01/1954	6/23/1969	7/09/1974	15
(71-11)	3/16/1955	9/23/1971	12/29/1971	16
	3/19/1957			
	3/19/1957	4/01/1962	11/26/1973	5
(70-17)	5/05/1959	7/03/1981		22
	4/11/1962			
	9/25/1962	7/25/1965		3
	8/11/1965	5/14/1969	4/05/1982	4
(69-11)	8/30/1967			
	10/04/1968			
	no action			

NAME	STATE	NAMED BY	AGE WHEN NOMINATED	ACTION
WARREN E. BURGER	Minn.	Nixon	61	Conf.
[Clement Haynsworth]	S.C.	Nixon	56	Rej.
[G. Harrold Carswell]	Fla.	Nixon	50	Rej.
Harry A. Blackmun	Minn.	Nixon	61	Conf.
Lewis F. Powell Jr.	Va.	Nixon	64	Conf.
William H. Rehnquist	Ariz.	Nixon	47	Conf.
John Paul Stevens	Ill.	Ford	55	Conf.
Sandra Day O'Connor	Ariz.	Reagan	51	Conf.

```
** CAPITALS  = Chief Justice
   BRACKETS  = Did not serve
   °         = Earlier court service
   *         = Earlier nomination not confirmed
```

Source: *The Supreme Court: Justice and the Law*, 3d ed., 1983, Congressional Quarterly Inc.

VOTE	DATE OF ACTION	DATE RESIGNED	DIED	YEARS ON COURT
(74-3)	6/09/1969			
(45-55)	11/21/1969			
(45-51)	4/08/1970			
(94-0)	5/12/1970			
(89-1)	12/06/1971			
(68-26)	12/10/1971			
(98-0)	12/17/1975			
(99-0)	9/21/1981			

Conf.	=	Confirmed
Rej.	=	Rejected
Dec.	=	Declined
Post	=	Postponed
W/draw	=	Withdrawn

(Where no vote is listed, confirmation was by voice or otherwise unrecorded vote.)

A Mini-Guide to
the Background Literature

There are literally thousands of books, articles, and judicial decisions broadly relevant to this book's subject. Believing that a selected bibliography would not be especially useful, I simply mention here several of the works that an interested reader might wish to consult as guides to the exploration of this vast terrain.

The authoritative collection of the records that remain from the convention that drafted the Constitution in 1787 is that edited by Max Farrand, *The Records of the Federal Convention of 1787* (New Haven: Yale University Press, 1937). For readers interested in exploring what the Supreme Court has made of the Constitution that emerged from that convention, my favorite collection of edited Supreme Court opinions and related secondary materials is William Lockhart, Yale Kamisar, and Jesse Choper, *Constitutional Law: Cases—Comments —Questions*, 5th ed. (St. Paul, Minn.: West Publishing Co., 1980). A much cited and quite comprehensive although somewhat controversial overview of constitutional law from 1789 to 1978 is my own treatise *American Constitutional Law* (Mineola, N.Y.: Foundation Press, 1978). Less technical and comprehensive and more current is my book *Constitutional Choices* (Cambridge, Mass.: Harvard University Press, 1985). For a dramatically different approach to constitutional interpretation, one urging a very narrow reading of the Fourteenth Amendment in particular, the reader might want to consult Raoul Berger, *Government by Judiciary* (Cambridge: Harvard University Press, 1977). Also of more than usual interest is a book by Jesse Choper, *Judicial Review and the National Political Process* (Chicago: University of Chicago Press, 1980), which urges a greater degree of judicial activism when the Supreme Court is called upon to protect individual rights than when it is asked to umpire contests between the national government and the states or within the national government itself. Especially lucid is a book by John Hart Ely, *Democracy and Distrust* (Cambridge: Harvard University Press, 1980), which urges judicial *restraint* on such substantive matters as rights of privacy and personal autonomy, but judicial *activism* in preserving the process of fair political representation—a distinction challenged in my book *Constitutional Choices*.

Turning from constitutional law to Supreme Court lore, one of the most readable one-volume histories of the Supreme Court as an institution is Leo Pfeffer, *This Honorable Court* (Boston: Beacon Press, 1965). A more elaborate (and highly pro-Federalist) history that will take the reader up to Chief Justice Taft is the classic three-volume study by Charles Warren, *The Supreme Court in United States History* (Boston: Little, Brown, 1922). A thoughtful volume that picks up where Warren leaves off is Alpheus Thomas Mason, *The Supreme Court from Taft to Burger* (Baton Rouge: Louisiana State University Press, 1979).

The leading collection of biographical essays on the individual Justices who served from 1789 to 1978, with excerpts from sample opinions by each, is the five-volume set edited by Leon Friedman and Fred Israel, *The Justices of the Supreme Court* (New York: Chelsea House, 1969–78). The leading political history of Supreme Court appointments is Henry Abraham, *Justices and Presidents*, 2d ed. (New York: Oxford University Press, 1985).

For an inside look at the work of the Warren Court, the best source is Bernard Schwartz, *Super Chief: Earl Warren and His Supreme Court* (New York: New York University Press, 1983). Although there is no real counterpart for the post-Warren years, a readable and usually reliable peek inside the Burger Court is provided by Bob Woodward and Scott Armstrong, *The Brethren* (New York: Simon & Schuster, 1979). An excellent and provocative collection of essays about the Burger Court's decisions is that edited by Vincent Blasi, *The Burger Court: The Counterrevolution That Wasn't* (New Haven: Yale University Press, 1983).

Index

ABOUT THE AUTHOR

LAURENCE TRIBE has taught at Harvard Law School since the age of twenty-seven, and holds Harvard's only chair in Constitutional Law. *Time* magazine named him one of the country's ten best law professors. *The National Law Journal* called him one of America's 100 most powerful lawyers in public or private life. His treatise *American Constitutional Law* received the Coif Award in 1980 for the most outstanding legal writing in the nation, and is widely said to be the leading modern work on the subject. Senators Gary Hart and Edward Kennedy say Tribe's book *Constitutional Choices*, published in 1985, secures Tribe's place "as the foremost constitutional thinker of our time" and as "America's preeminent practitioner and scholar of constitutional law."

Author of twelve other books and over ninety articles, and a frequent expert witness before Congress, Tribe also has won many important Supreme Court victories. *The National Law Journal* said in 1984 that Tribe had compiled a better record there "than any other attorney after the U.S. Solicitor General." According to *The American Lawyer*, many a "hopeless case" has ended up in Tribe's "long string of successes" because he "probably knows the mind of the Court better than any other advocate now appearing before it."